THE JOY OF SIGNING PUZZLE BOOK 2

Linda Lascelle Hillebrand
with Lottie L. Riekehof

Gospel Publishing House
Springfield, Missouri
02-0538

To my best friend, Tim

All words needed for the puzzles can be found in *The Joy of Signing*, Second Edition, by Lottie L. Riekehof, and published by Gospel Publishing House, Springfield, Missouri 65802-1894 (ISBN 0-88243-520-5). All signs are used by permission.

Also available is the first *Joy of Signing Puzzle Book* (order number 02-0676).

2nd Printing 2001

International Standard Book Number 0-88243-538-8

Printed in the United States of America

Table of Contents

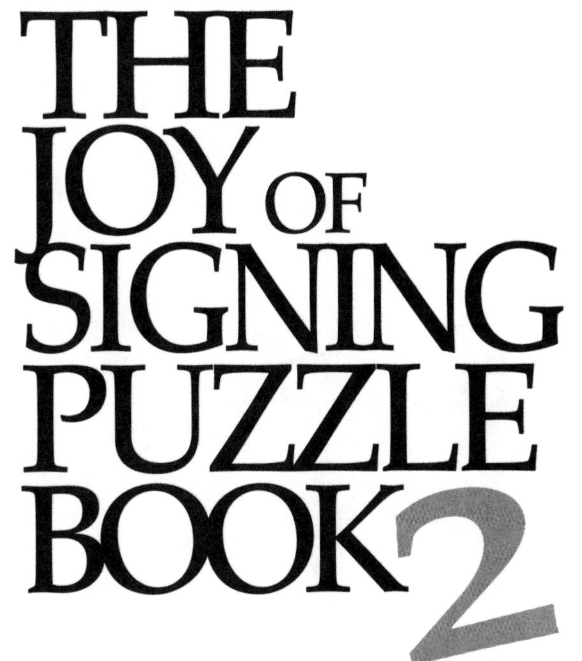

Manual Alphabet Chart

A 

B 

C 

D 

E 

F 

G 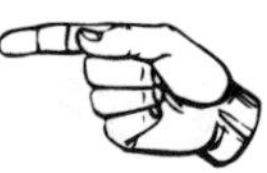

H 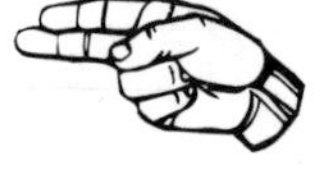

I 

J 

K 

L 

M 

N 

O 

P 

Q 

R 

S 

T 

U 

V 

W 

X 

Y 

Z 

Puzzles Chart

Chapter	Crossword Easy	Crossword Medium	Finger/Words Easy	Seek-A-Word Easy	Seek-A-Word Medium	Pick-A-Word Easy	Origin Medium
1		●	● (Basic)				
2	●				●		
3	●				●		
4		●		●			
5			● (Easy)				●
6		●		●			
7	●				●		
8		●				●	
9	●						●
10		●	● (Basic)				
11	●				●		
12		●				●	
13	●						●
14		●	● (Scrambled)				
15			● (Easy)				●
16		●		●			
17			● (Scrambled)				●
18	●				●		
19		●		●			
20	●	●					
21			● (Easy)				●
22					●	●	
23			● (Basic)				●
24		●				●	
25					●	●	

Introduction

Whether you are learning sign language to communicate with a family member, coworker, student, or friend—or just for fun—learning this beautiful, expressive language is an interesting and rewarding challenge.

For hearing persons learning sign language, reading the origin in *The Joy of Signing* is a big advantage. These origins help the learner to understand why a sign is made a certain way, therefore making that sign much easier to remember.

The Joy of Signing Puzzle Book 2 includes a new puzzle known as the "Origin Puzzle," matching the origin with the fingerspelled and signed version of a word. This book is a combination of both easy and medium level puzzles. Medium level puzzles often use words that are listed second, third, or fourth, such as afraid, **"scared,""frightened,"** and **"terrify."**

We hope you find enjoyment and satisfaction while you play and learn.

Pick-A-Word Puzzles

Pick-A-Word puzzles are made up of signs and their spelled-out meanings. Printed to the right of each sign are three words. Underline the correct one.

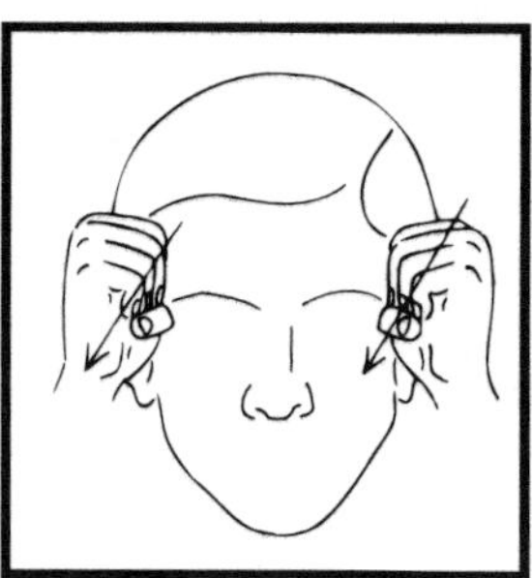

A. Easter

B. <u>Education</u>

C. Expression

Finger/Word Puzzles

Finger/Word puzzles are a combination of fingerspelling and actual signs. The following three types are included in this book.

Basic Finger/Words

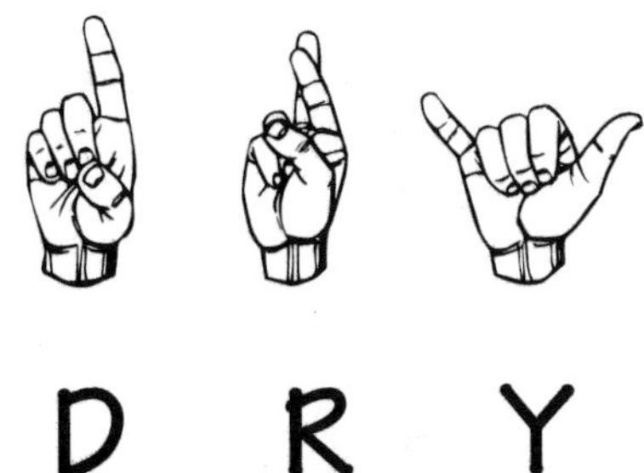

The fingerspelling for each sign is in the correct order. Write the correct letter below each hand position.

Scrambled Finger/Words

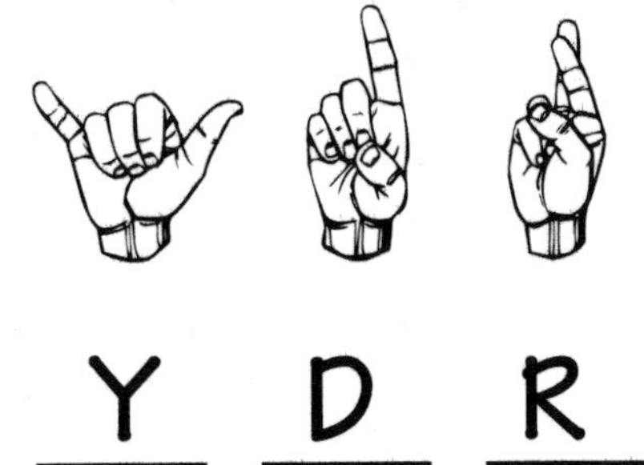

The fingerspelling for each sign is scrambled. Write the correct letter below each hand position and then unscramble the letters to form the correct word for each sign.

Easy Finger/Words

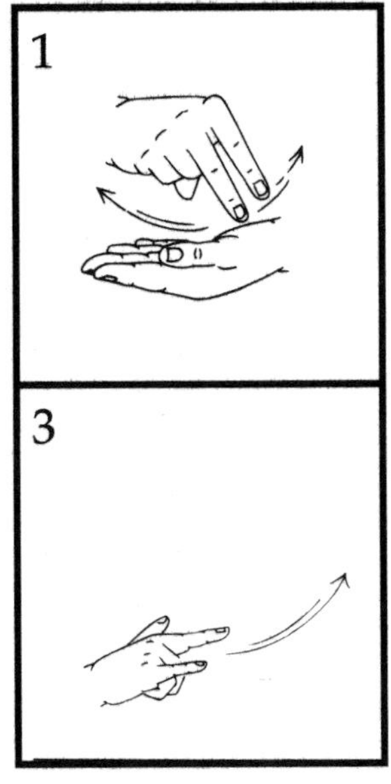

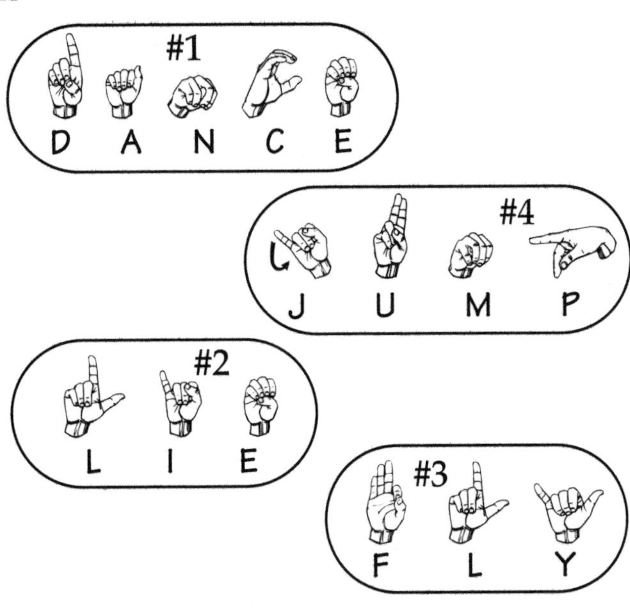

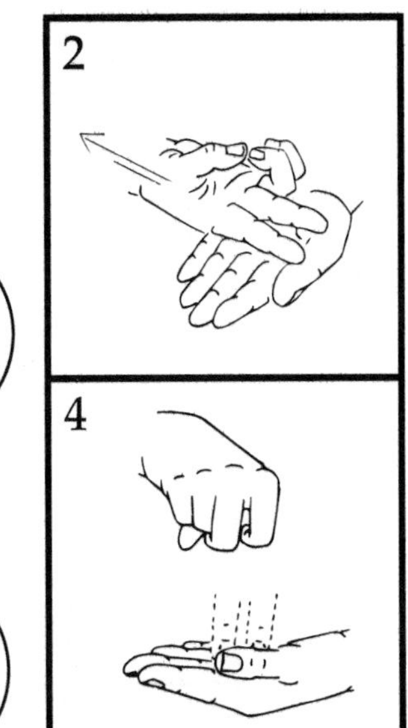

The fingerspelling for each sign is in the correct order; however, the corresponding word is *not* found next to the sign itself. Locate the fingerspelled version for each sign pictured. Circle it, number it, and write the letters of the word underneath.

Seek-A-Word Puzzles

Seek-A-Word puzzles are comprised of signs and their spelled-out meanings, which are found somewhere in the puzzle. The words may be written vertically, horizontally, diagonally, forward, or backward. The easy level puzzles use the printed alphabet while the medium level puzzles use the manual alphabet.

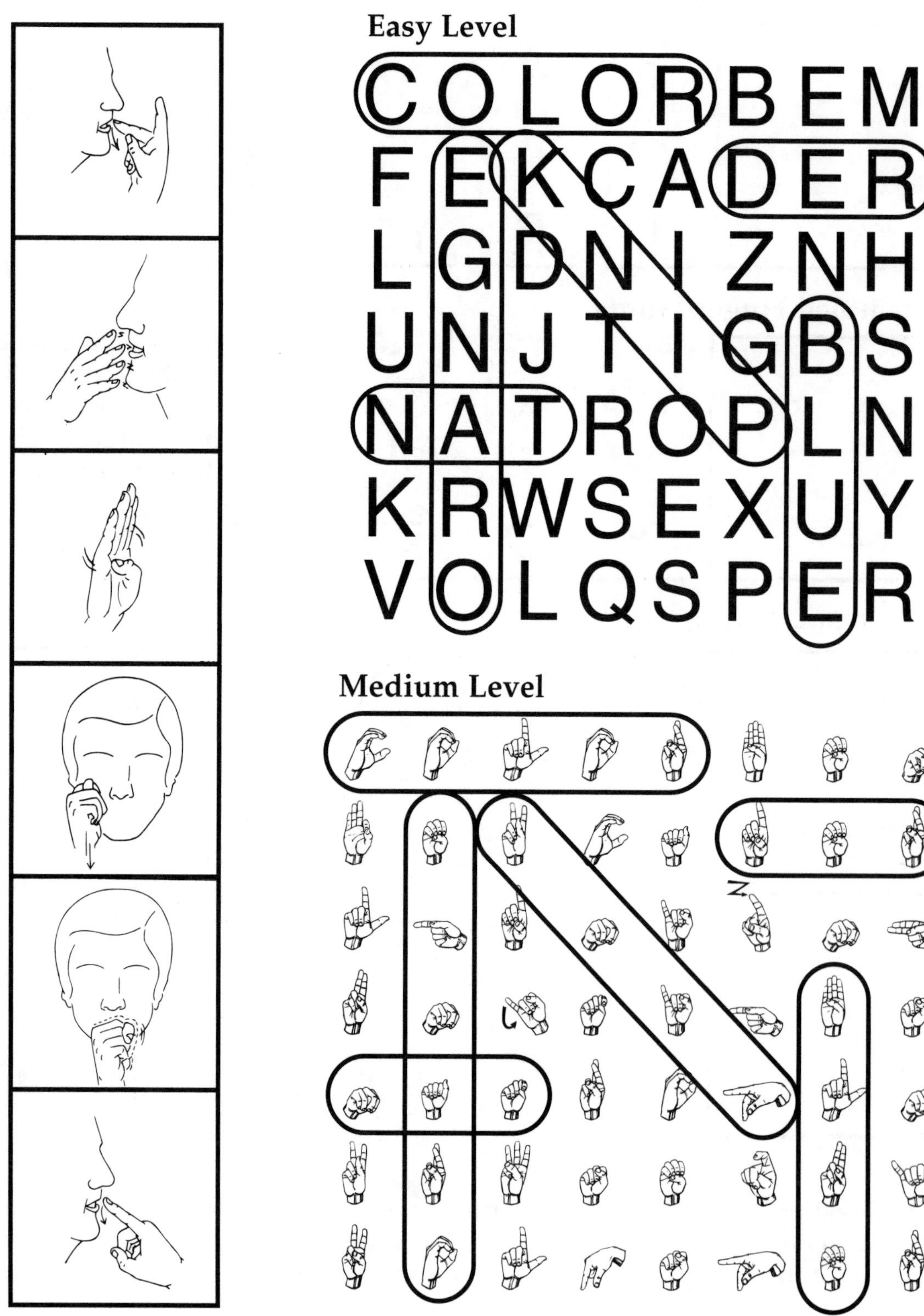

Crossword Puzzles

Crossword puzzles are comprised of signs and their spelled-out meanings. Each easy level puzzle has less than twenty words, while each medium level puzzle can have as many as forty-two words.

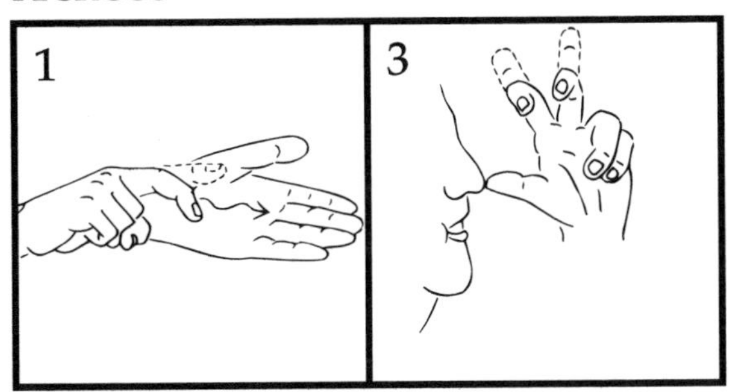

DOWN

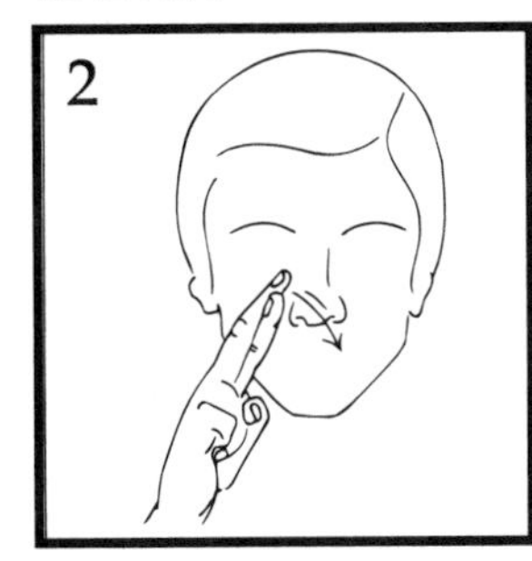

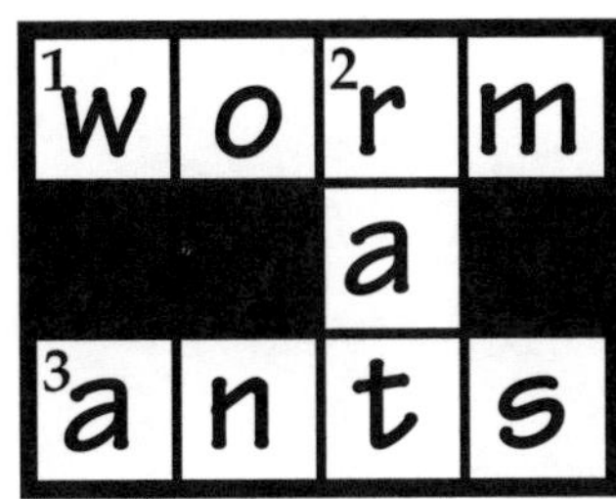

Note: If a sign's spelled-out meaning has an apostrophe, hyphen, or space, it should be omitted. For example,"narrow-minded" becomes "narrowminded," "let go" becomes "letgo," and "don't" becomes "dont."

Origin Puzzles

Origin puzzles are comprised of signs and fingerspelling. Match the sign with its origin and the fingerspelled word. Write the number (sign) and the letter (origin) in the corresponding fingerspelled box.

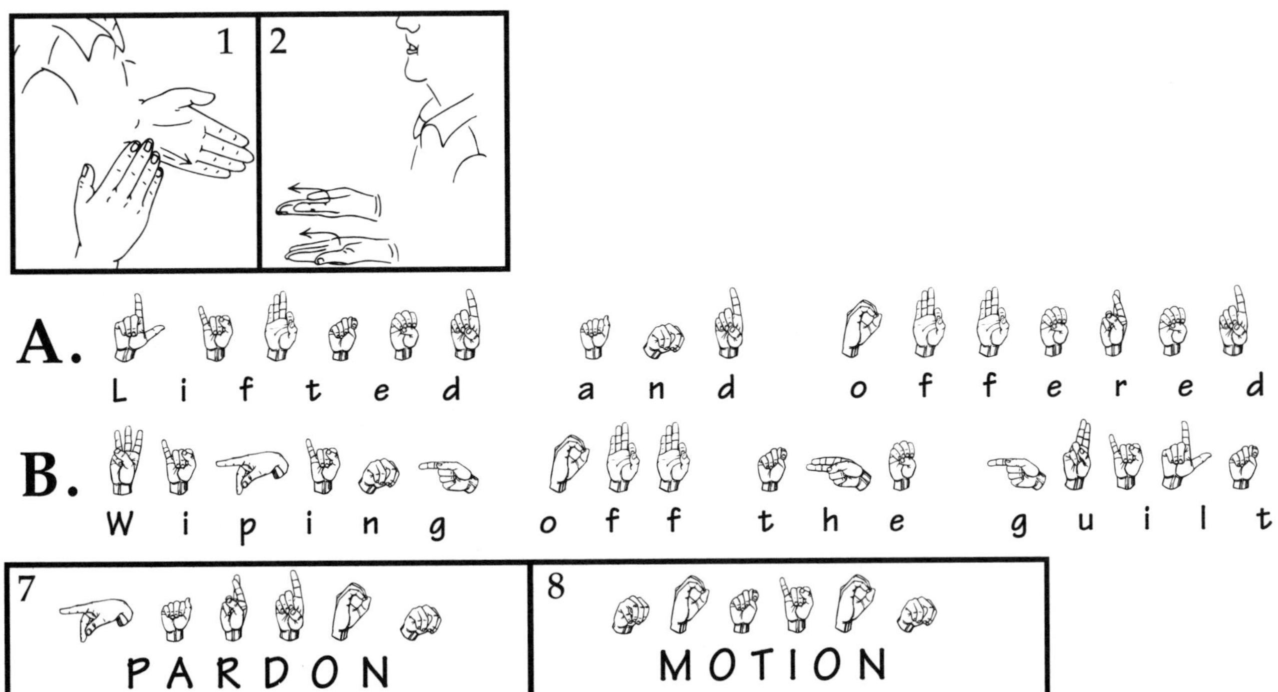

Chapter 1

Family Relationships

Spell the word for the sign given; write the letter below each hand position.

1 ___ ___ ___

2 ___ ___ ___ ___

3 ___ ___ ___

4 ___ ___ ___ ___ ___

5 ___ ___ ___ ___ ___

6 ___ ___ ___

6 ___ ___ ___ ___

7 ___ ___ ___ ___ ___

8 ___ ___ ___ ___

9 ___ ___ ___

10 ___ ___ ___ ___ ___

11 ___ ___ ___ ___

Chapter 1

Across
1
4
8
10
11
12
13
15
16
17
18
24
Or
25
27
29
30
32
Down
2
3
5
6
7
8
9
14
19
Or
20
21
22
23
26
28
31

Family Relationships

On the previous page, write the meaning for each sign given. Then fill in the appropriate blanks in the crossword puzzle on this page.

Chapter 2
Pronouns, Question Words, & Endings

ACROSS

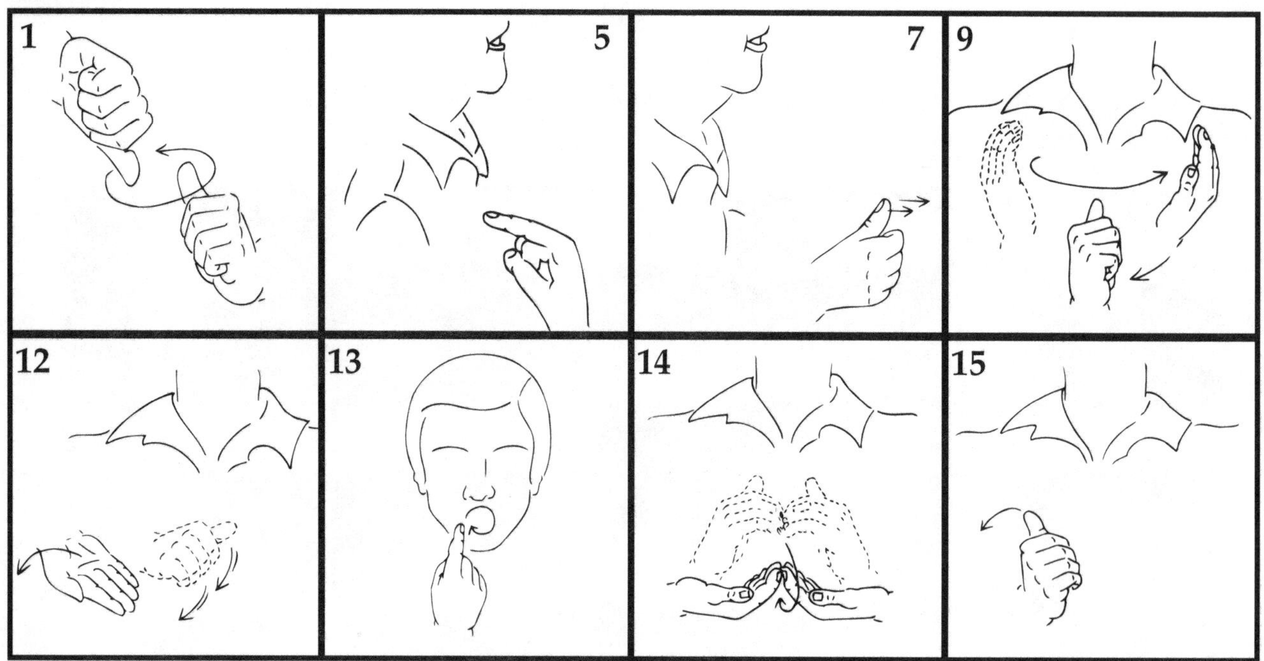

DOWN

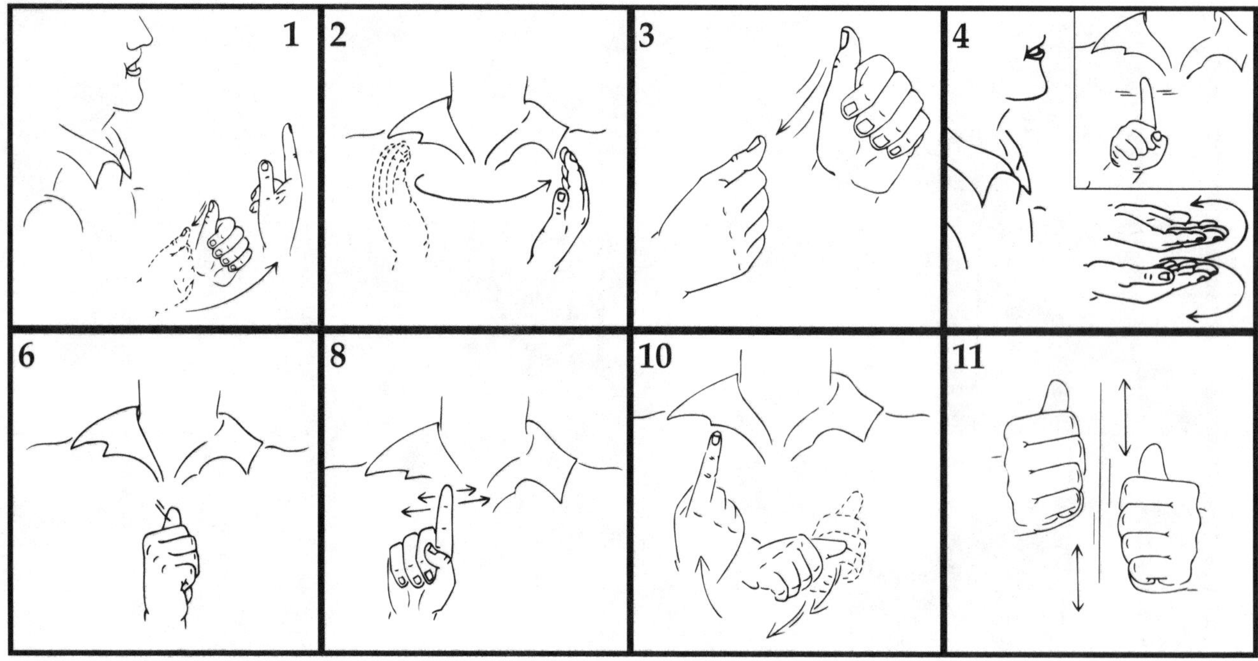

On the previous page, write the meaning for each sign given. Then fill in the appropriate blanks in the crossword puzzle on this page.

Chapter 2

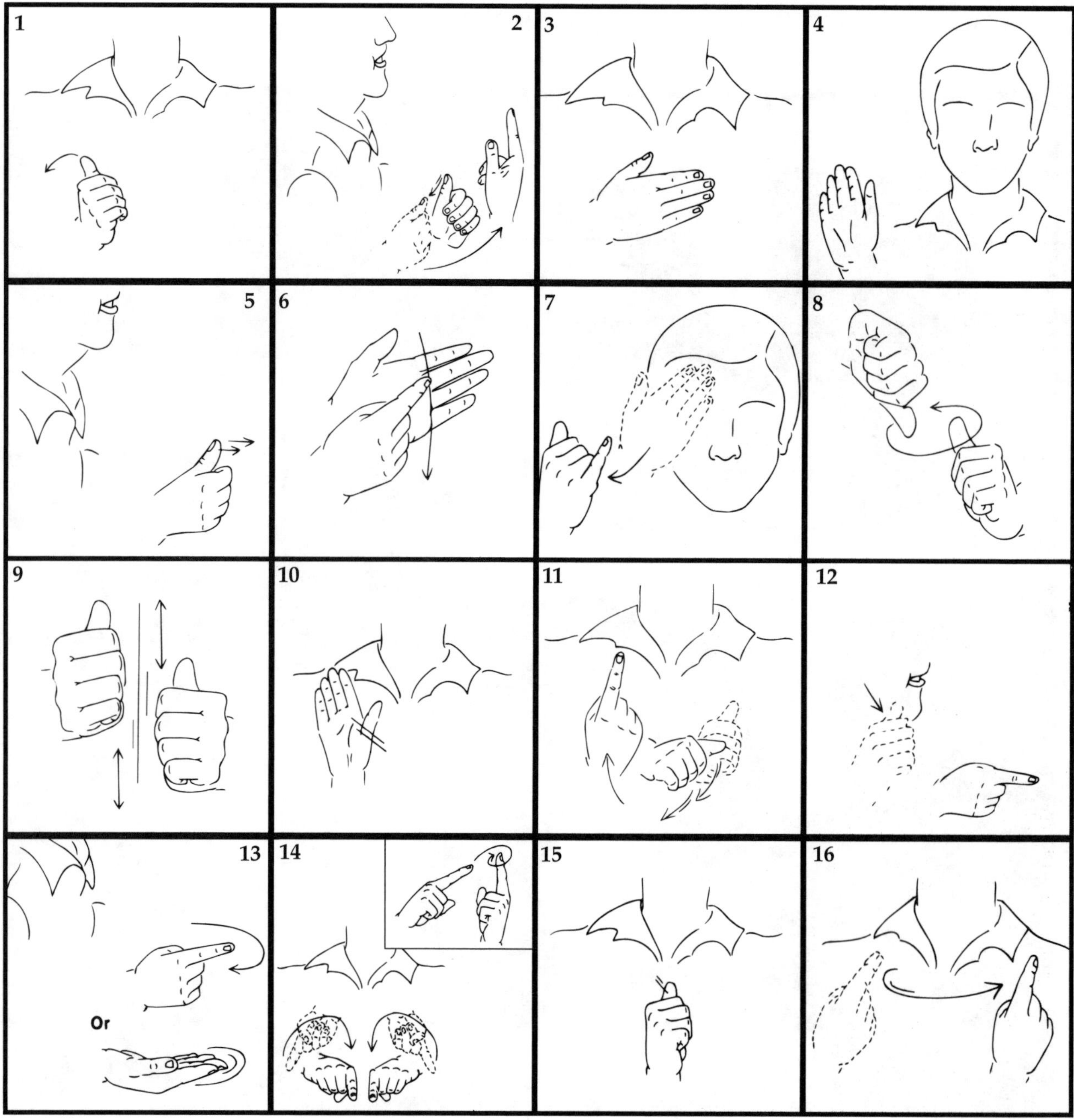

Pronouns, Question Words, & Endings

On the previous page, write the meaning for each sign. Then find the words in the seek-a-word puzzle. The words may read forward, backward, up, down, or diagonally.

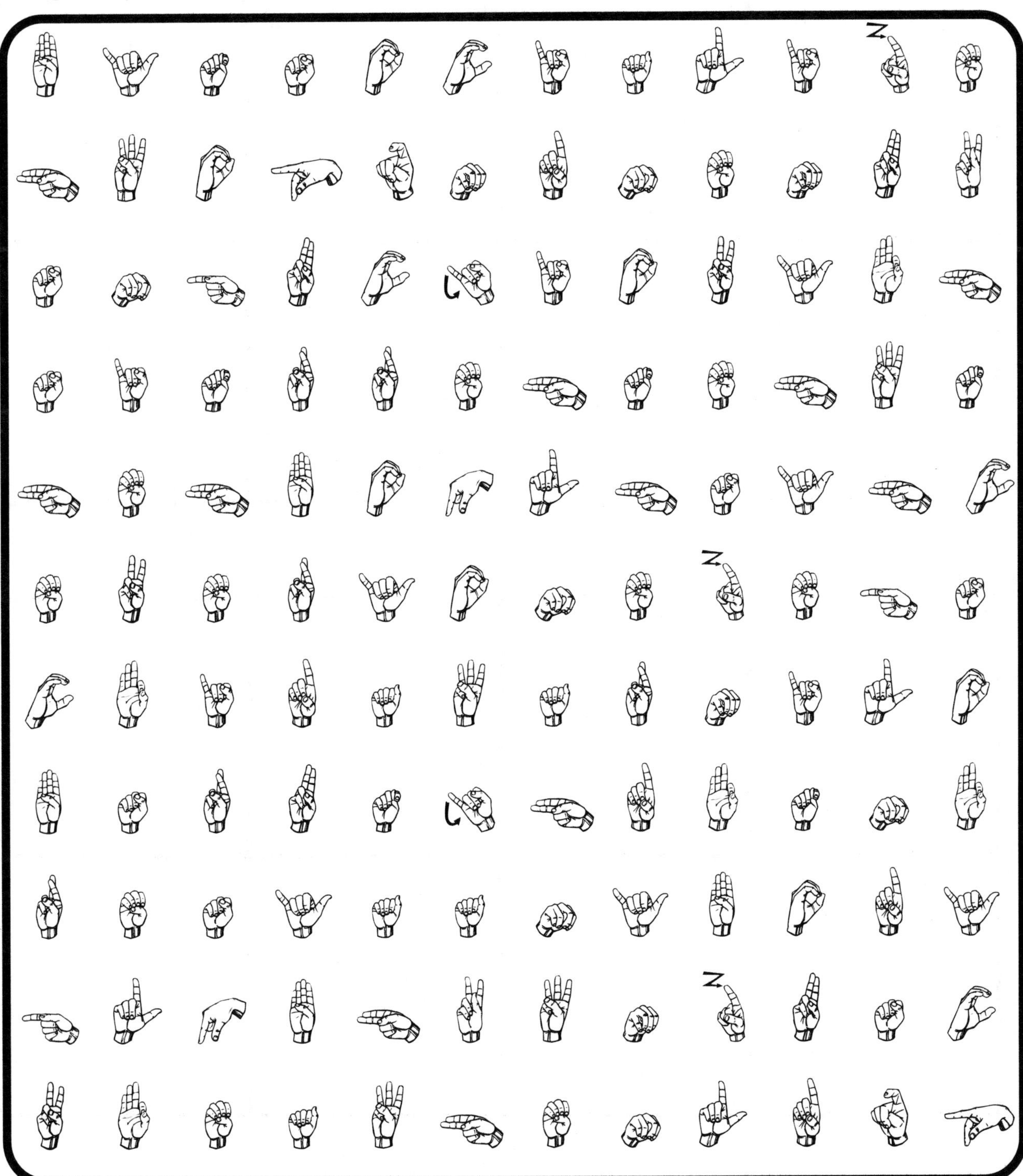

Chapter 3

Time

Across

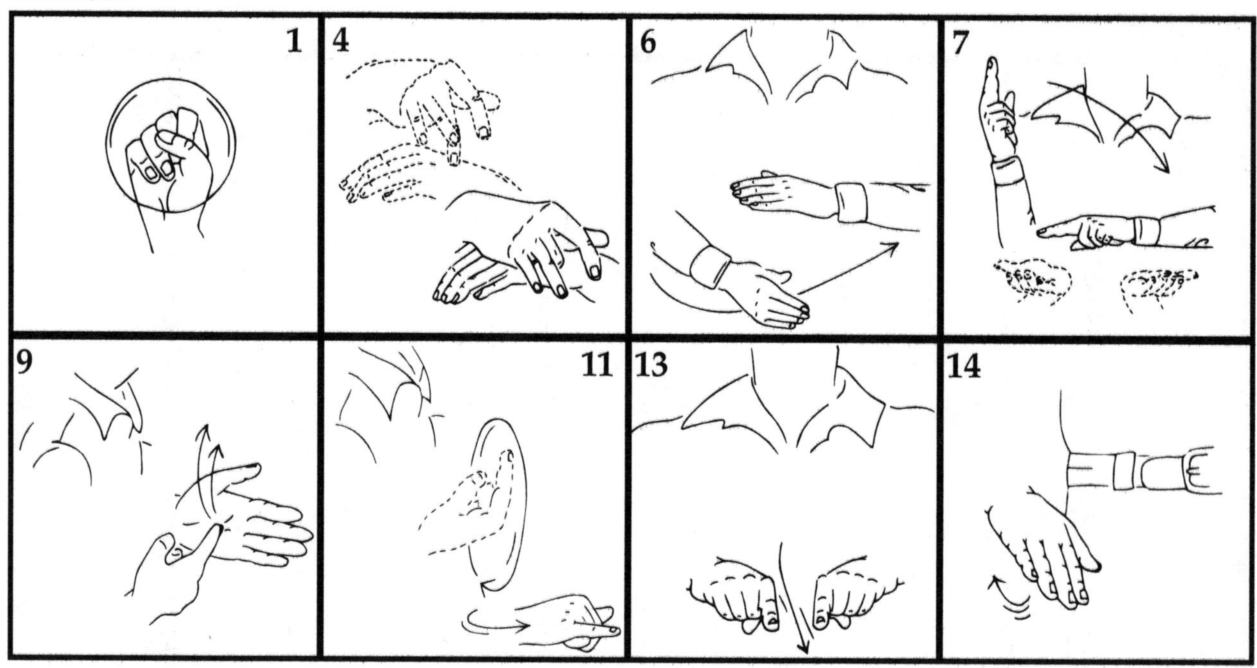

Down

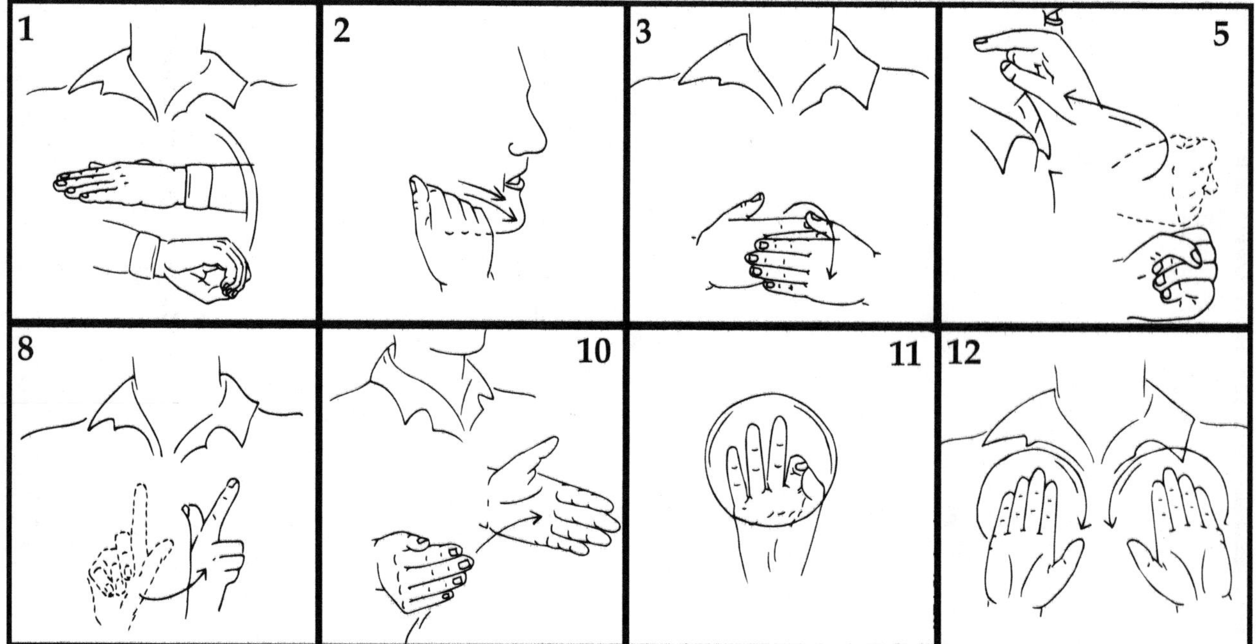

On the previous page, write the meaning for each sign given. Then fill in the appropriate blanks in the crossword puzzle on this page.

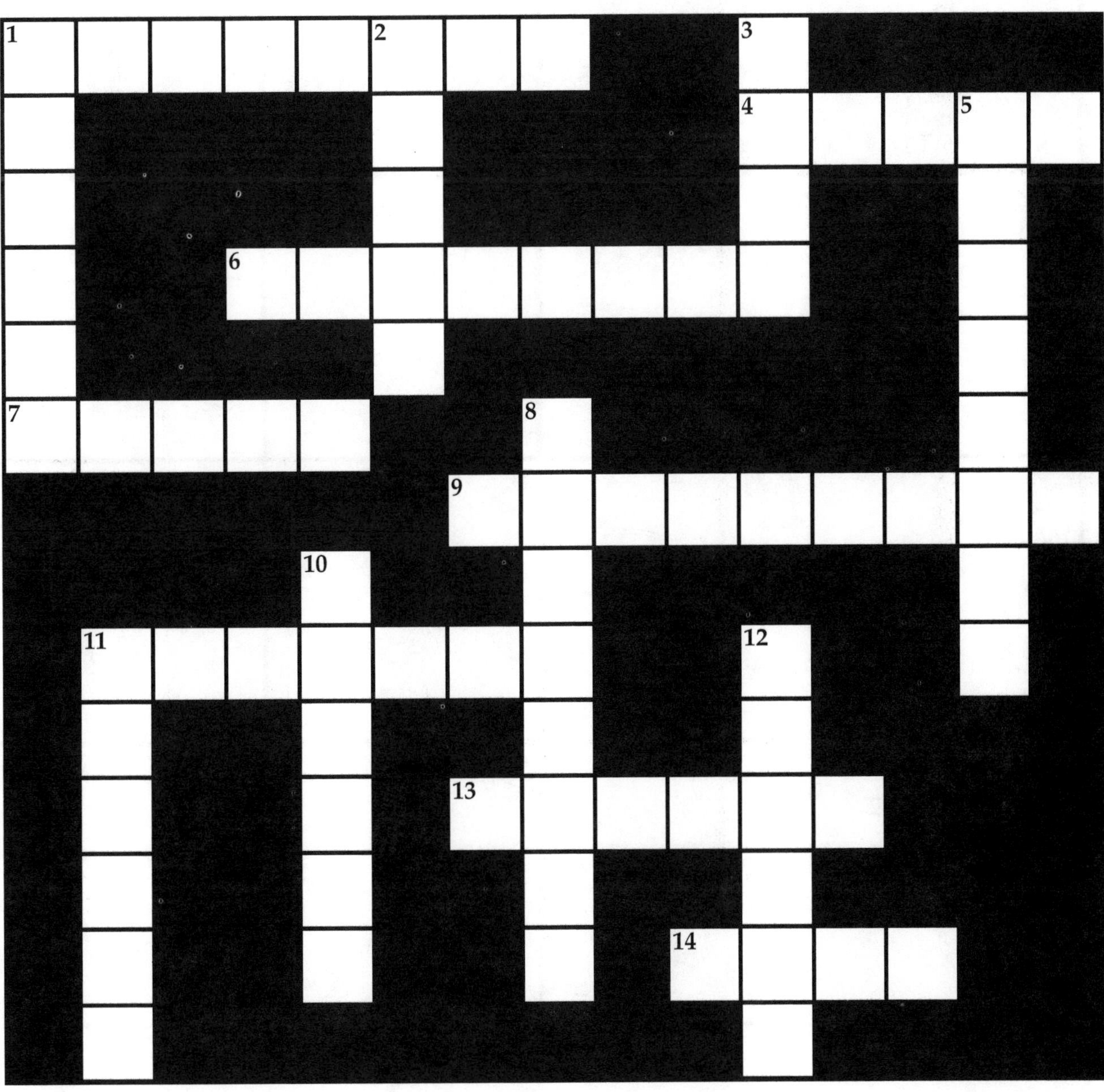

Chapter 3

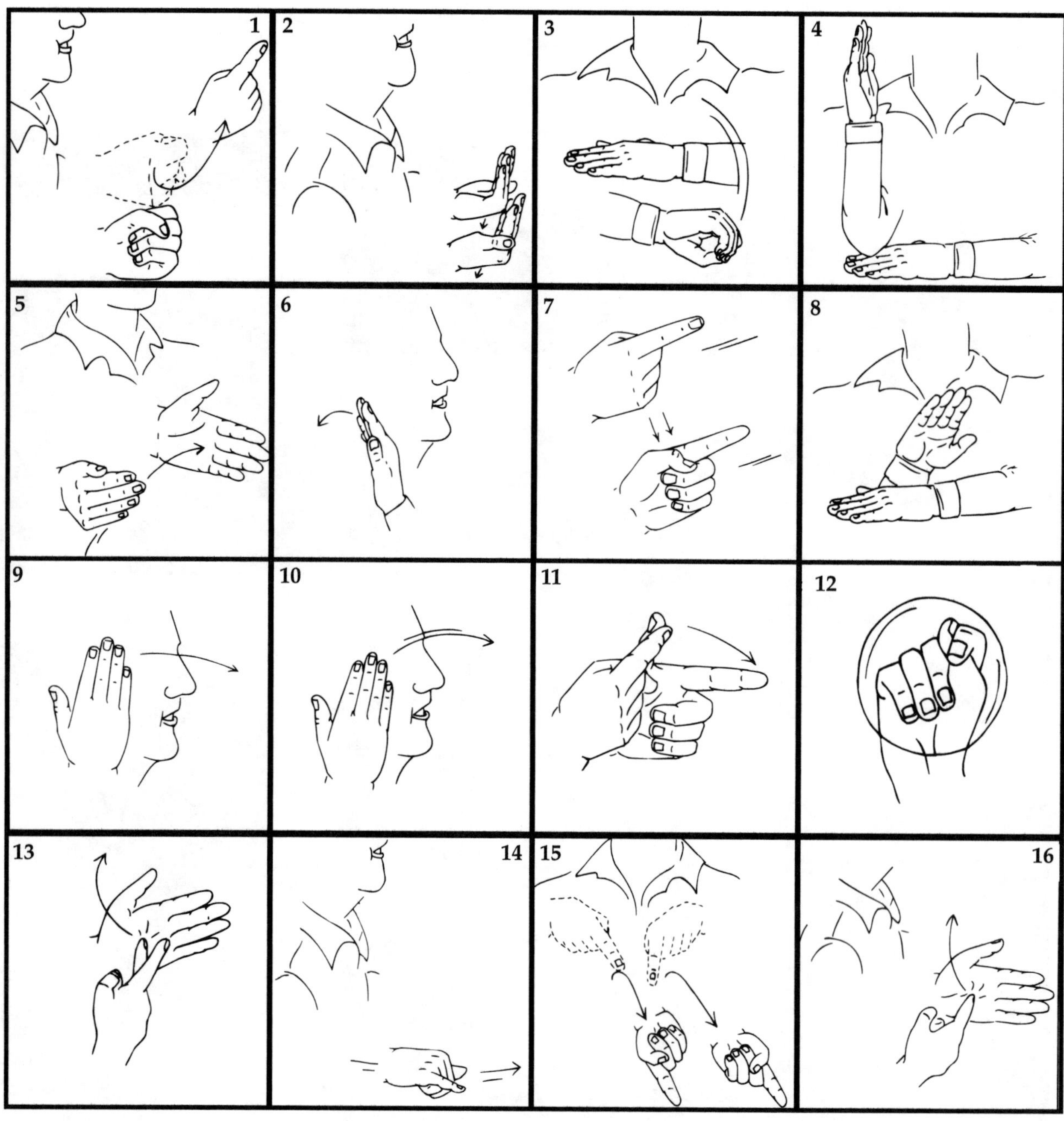

Time

On the previous page, write the meaning for each sign. Then find the words in the seek-a-word puzzle. The words may read forward, backward, up, down, or diagonally.

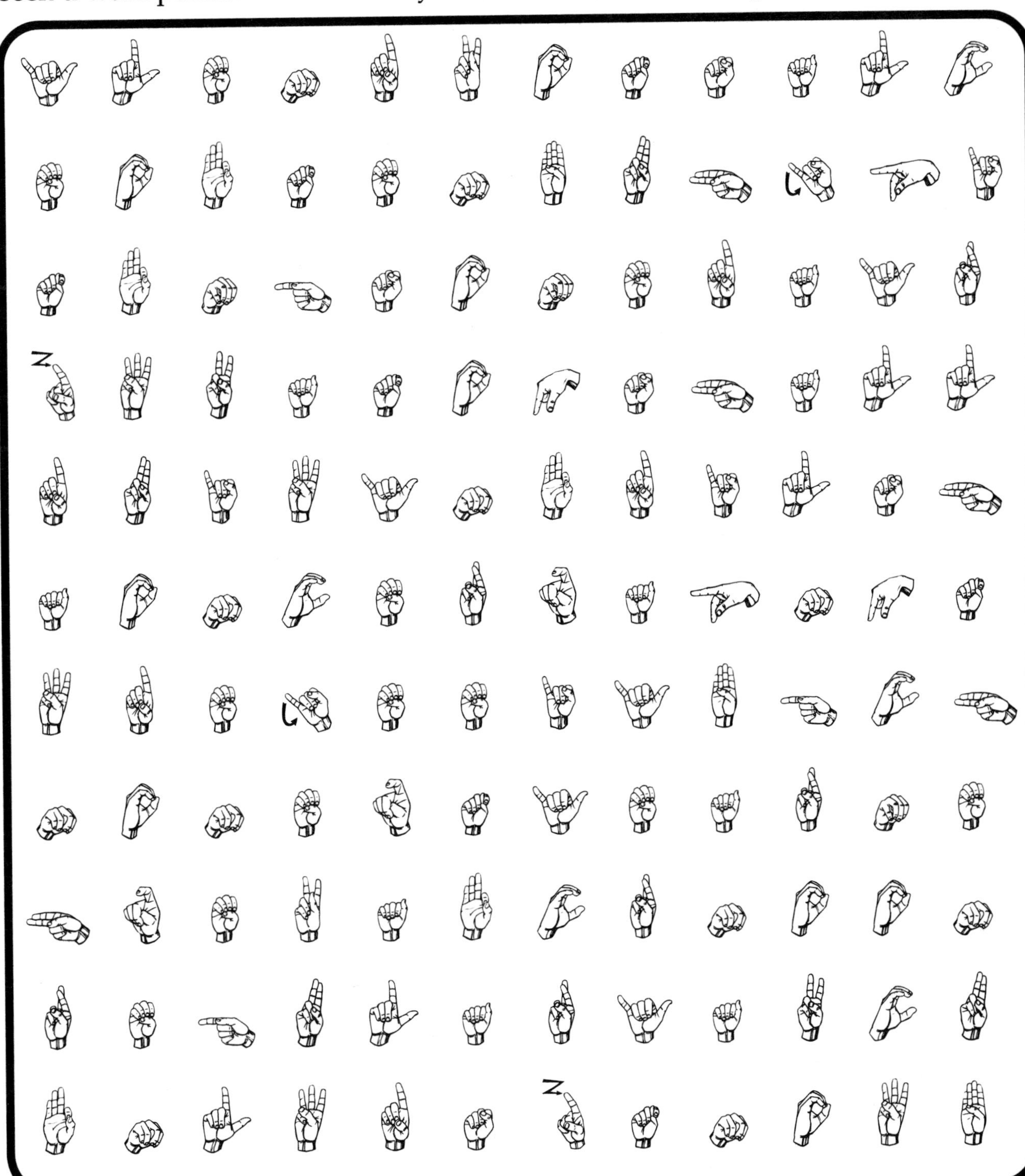

Chapter 4

Mental Action

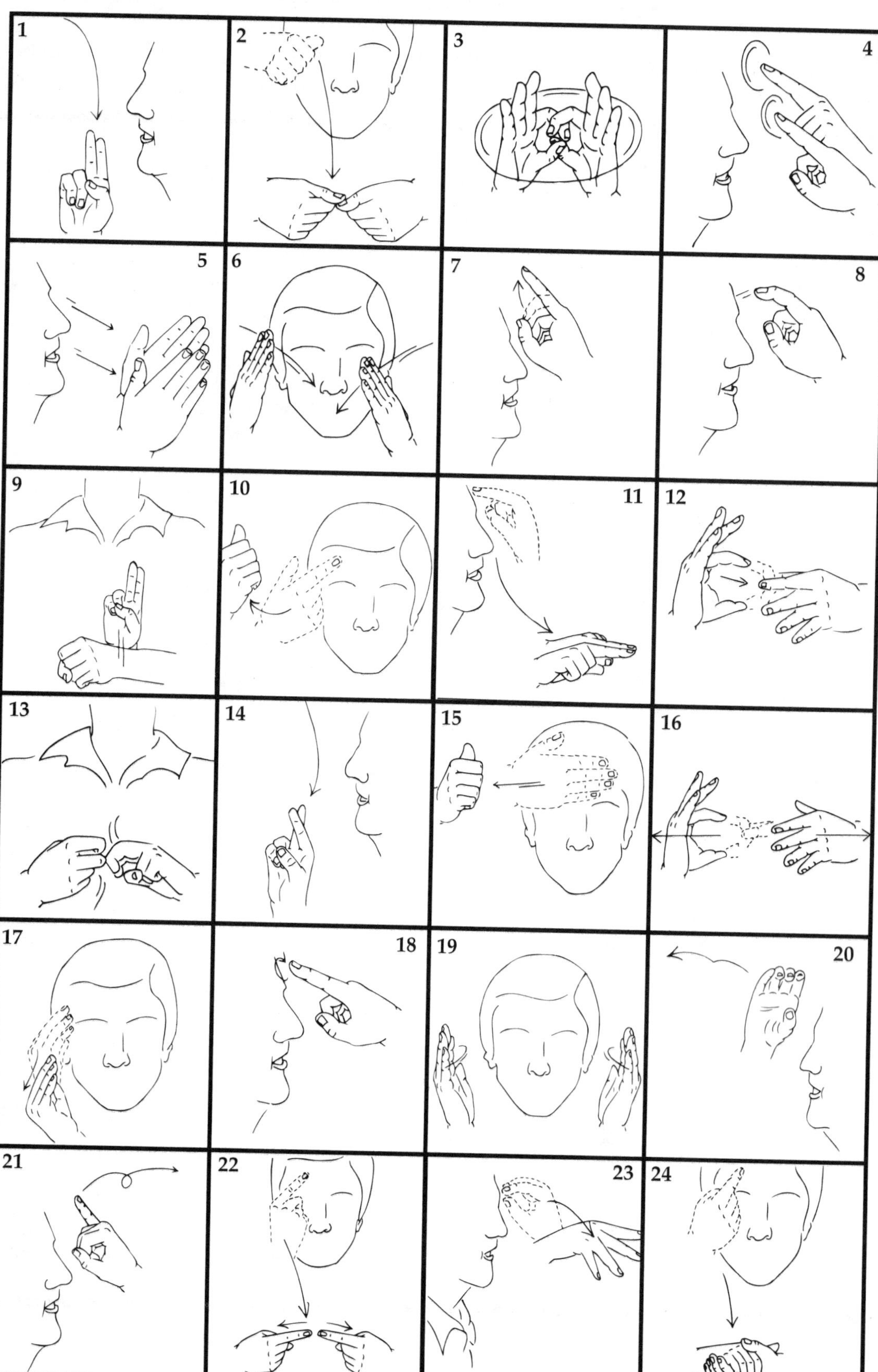

On the previous page, write the meaning for each sign. Then find the words in the seek-a-word puzzle. The words may read forward, backward, up, down, or diagonally.

G	B	E	C	A	U	S	E	M	E	L	B	O	R	P
C	A	W	J	P	A	N	H	U	C	O	Q	Z	C	U
O	M	E	E	I	M	A	G	I	N	A	T	I	O	N
M	Y	R	R	O	W	B	O	D	E	H	O	N	O	R
P	F	E	A	E	G	X	D	N	I	M	D	G	P	L
A	K	S	C	Y	M	I	B	N	R	B	F	R	E	V
R	N	P	T	I	W	E	K	Q	E	T	H	T	R	J
E	O	E	N	P	J	F	M	L	P	N	G	E	A	O
W	I	C	O	C	L	V	I	B	X	O	V	E	T	I
C	T	T	D	X	S	E	P	R	E	H	S	R	I	N
J	N	S	A	E	V	K	M	Y	L	R	O	G	O	U
T	E	Y	G	E	U	N	D	E	R	S	T	A	N	D
L	T	I	R	M	Q	C	Y	L	L	A	U	S	U	N
R	T	P	E	C	N	O	C	Z	E	K	T	I	L	D
B	A	T	E	G	R	O	F	A	W	O	N	D	E	R

Chapter 4

ACROSS

1 4 8 10 11 12

14 18 19 23 25 26

29 31 32 34 35 36 Or

DOWN

1 2 3 4 Or 5 6

7 9 13 15 16 17

19 20 21 22 24 27

28 30 31 33

Mental Action

On the previous page, write the meaning for each sign given. Then fill in the appropriate blanks in the crossword puzzle on this page.

Chapter 5

Emotion and Feeling

Find the fingerspelled word for each sign given. Circle it, write the letters of the word underneath it, and write the corresponding number.

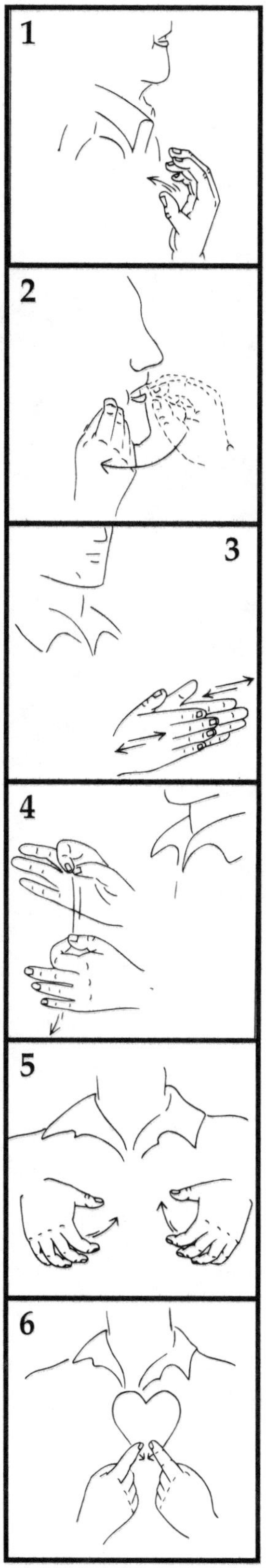

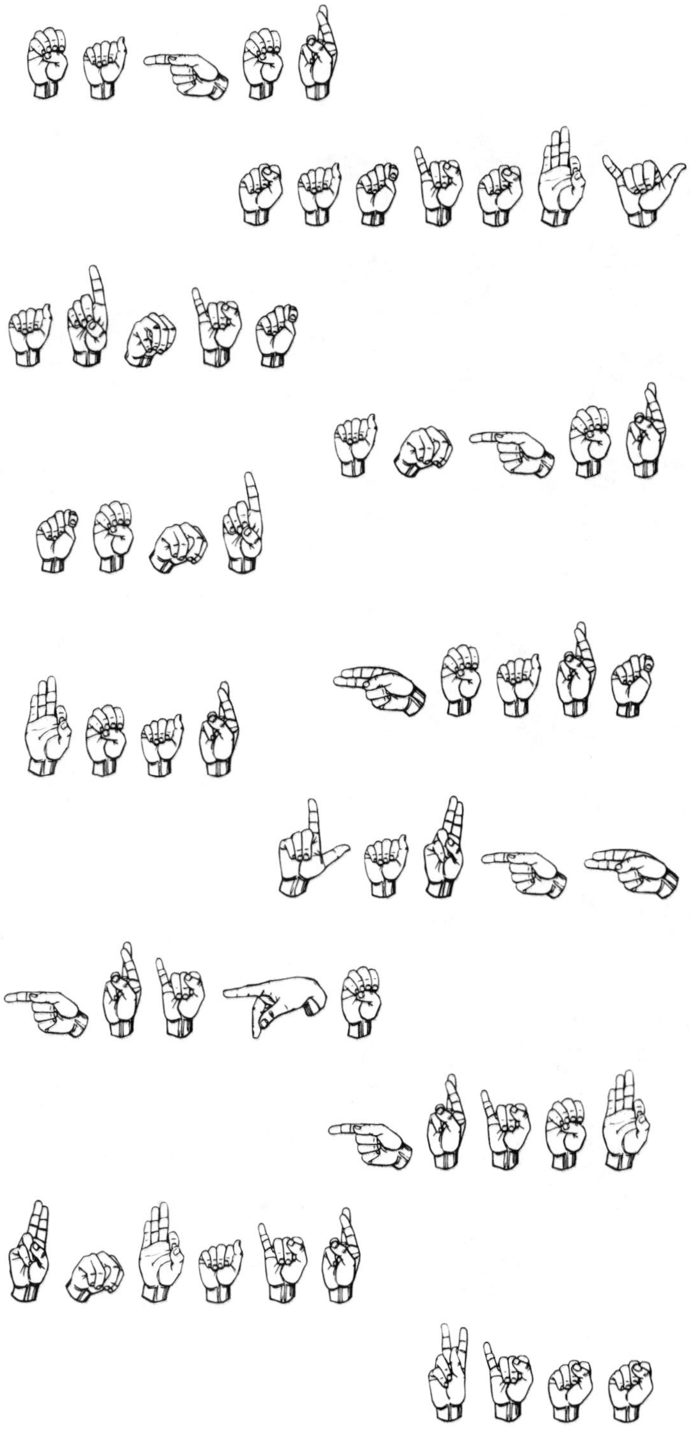

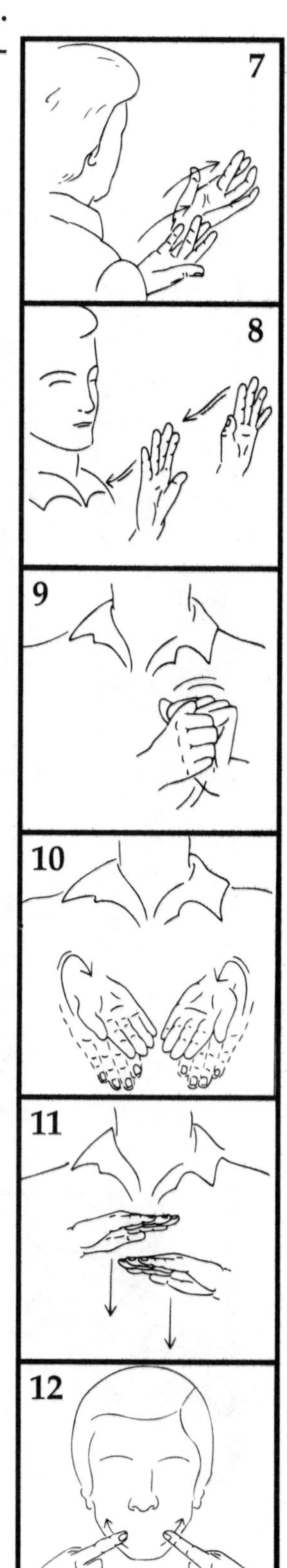

Match the sign with its origin and the fingerspelled word. Write the number (sign) and the letter (origin) in the corresponding fingerspelled box.

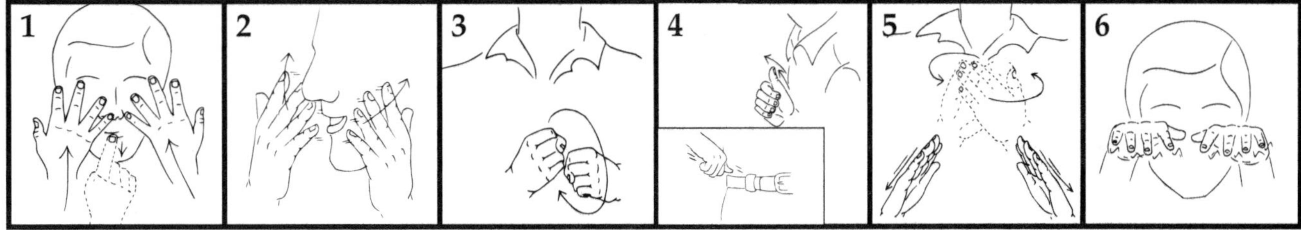

A.

B.

C.

D.

E.

F. 

7	8	9
______ ______	______ ______	______ ______
10	**11**	**12**
______ ______	______ ______	______ ______

Chapter 6
People, Occupations, and Money

On the previous page, write the meaning for each sign. Then find the words in the seek-a-word puzzle. The words may read forward, backward, up, down, or diagonally.

P	S	D	I	S	M	I	S	S	E	D	M	H	I	G
F	A	E	B	E	Q	H	T	V	B	R	A	Y	L	I
W	N	I	S	L	A	P	I	C	N	I	R	P	D	F
M	E	S	N	L	D	S	H	W	U	C	C	O	N	L
S	E	E	W	T	N	B	R	O	L	E	H	C	A	B
A	U	C	H	E	A	P	X	R	Y	V	C	R	J	U
I	Q	G	P	R	E	K	O	R	B	S	O	I	N	S
L	D	X	E	A	L	T	G	O	T	K	M	T	U	I
O	E	M	B	T	C	A	H	B	R	R	M	E	F	N
R	A	U	D	I	E	N	C	E	Q	J	U	Z	K	E
C	P	R	X	N	V	I	M	F	A	Y	N	L	C	S
N	E	T	R	E	A	S	U	R	E	R	I	O	E	S
A	V	Z	O	B	W	H	L	J	P	K	T	K	H	R
L	A	U	D	I	V	I	D	N	I	H	Y	E	C	O
C	S	N	W	O	R	C	L	P	C	H	A	N	G	E

Chapter 6

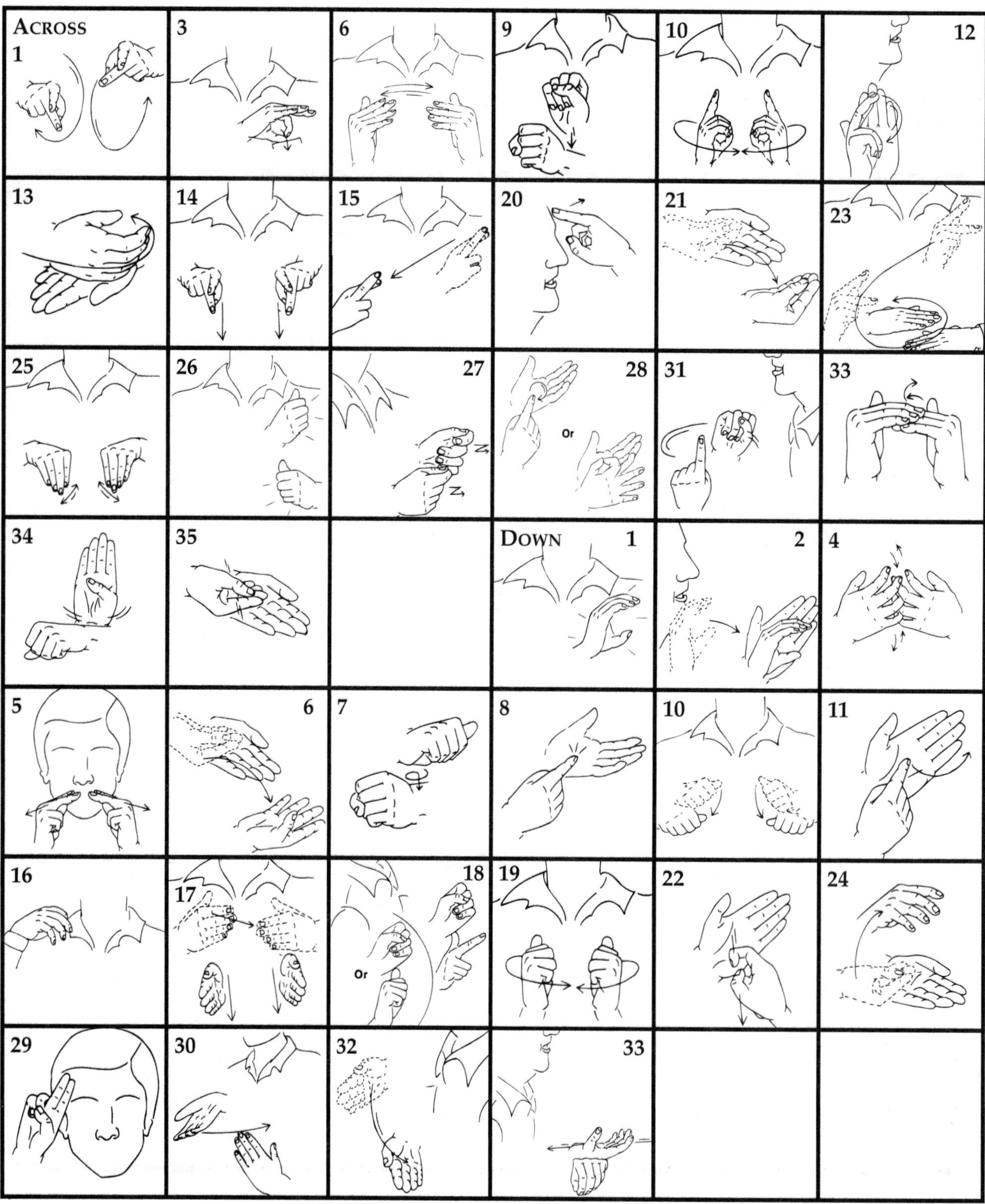
ACROSS
1
3
6
9
10
12
13
14
15
20
21
23
25
26
27
28
Or
31
33
34
35
DOWN
1
2
4
5
6
7
8
10
11
16
17
18
Or
19
22
24
29
30
32
33

People, Occupations, and Money

On the previous page, write the meaning for each sign given. Then fill in the appropriate blanks in the crossword puzzle on this page.

Chapter 7
Physical Movement and Travel

Across

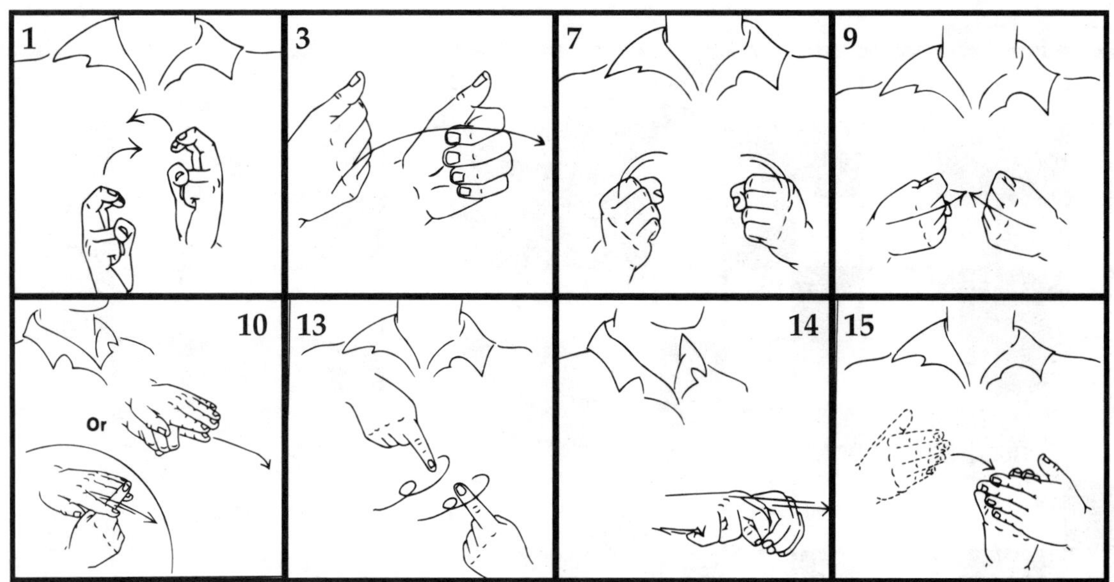

Down

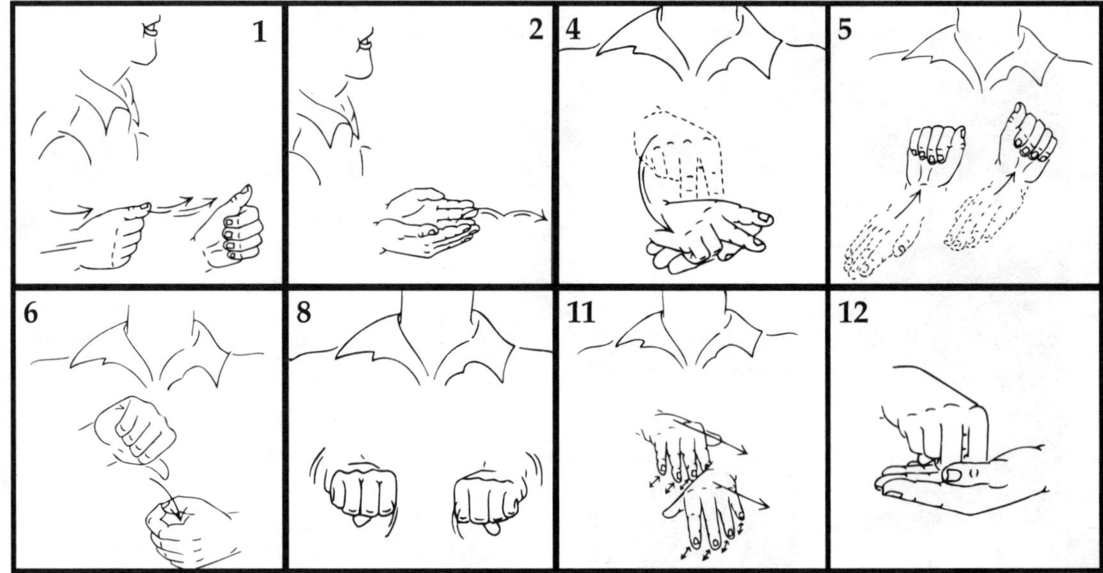

On the previous page, write the meaning for each sign given. Then fill in the appropriate blanks in the crossword puzzle on this page.

Chapter 7

Physical Movement and Travel

On the previous page, write the meaning for each sign. Then find the words in the seek-a-word puzzle. The words may read forward, backward, up, down, or diagonally.

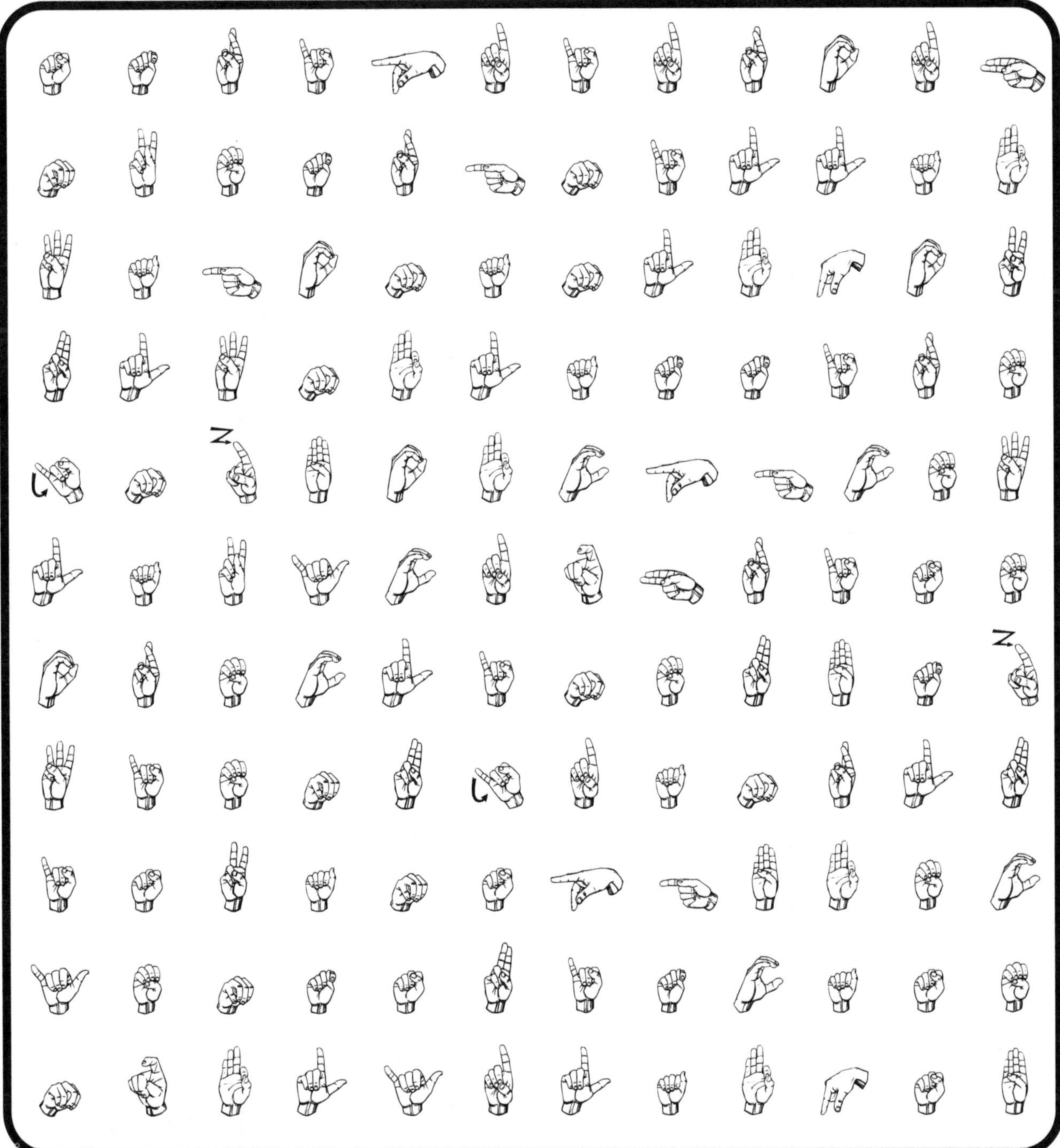

Chapter 8

Opposites

Underline the word that matches the given sign.

1 
A. From Now On
B. Always
C. Simple

2 
A. Up
B. Out
C. Tall

3 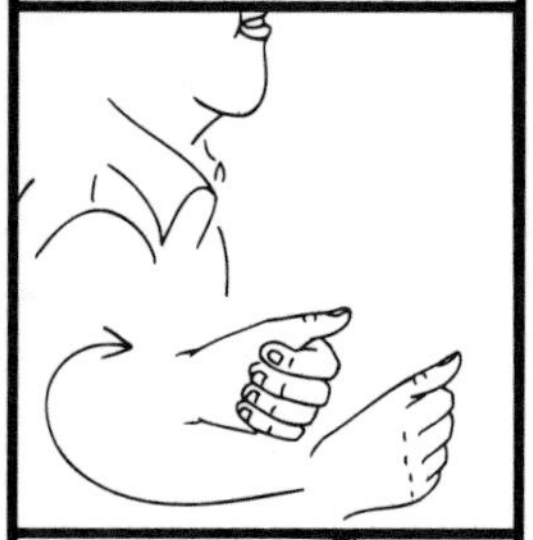
A. Last
B. Deteriorate
C. Behind

4 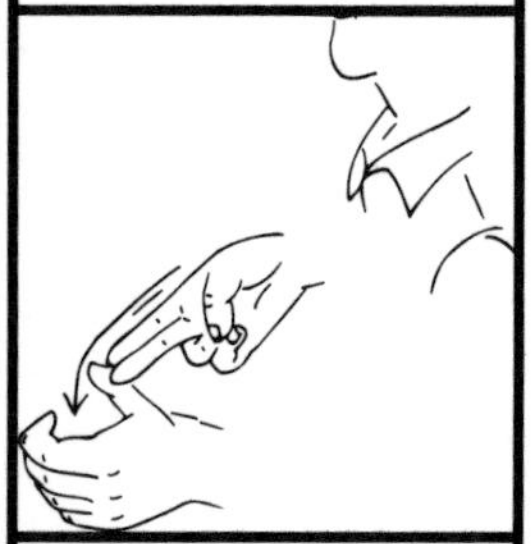
A. In
B. Join
C. Condense

5 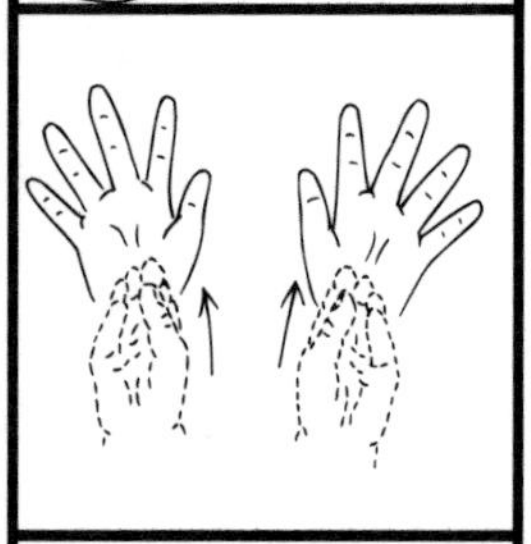
A. Open
B. Lights On
C. Set Up

6 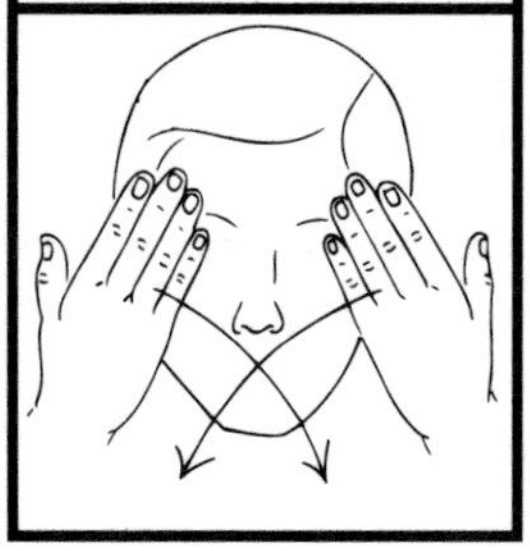
A. Worsen
B. Disappear
C. Dark

7 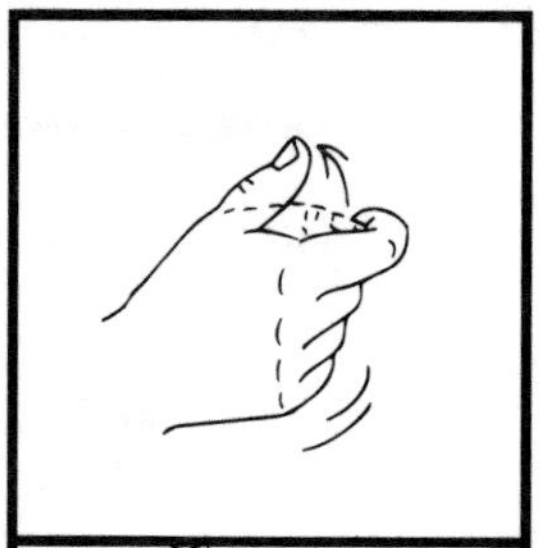
A. Open
B. Quick
C. Up

8 
A. Ask
B. Come
C. Assume

9 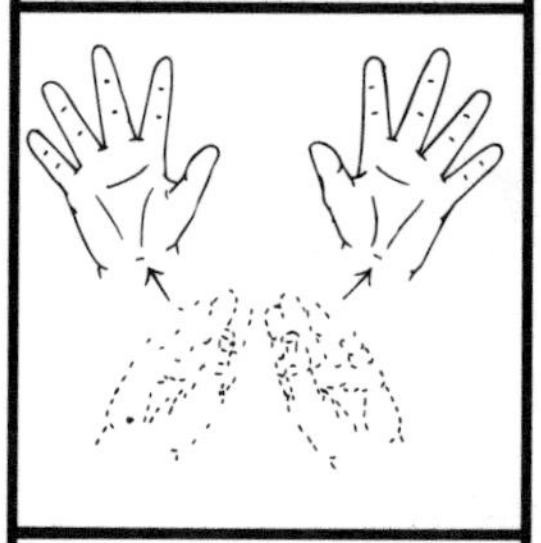
A. Expand
B. Light
C. Open

10 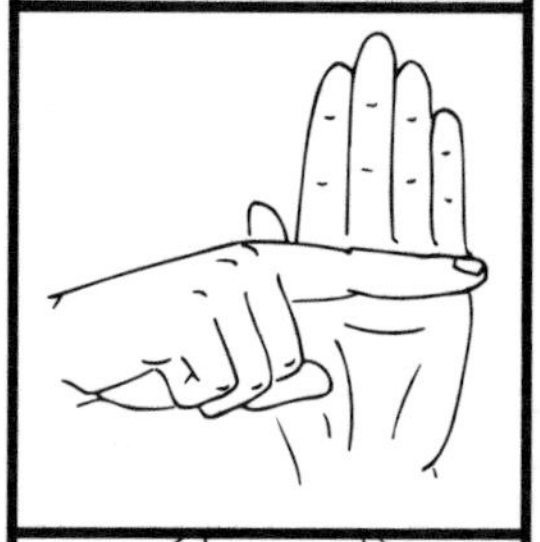
A. Can't
B. First
C. Negative

11 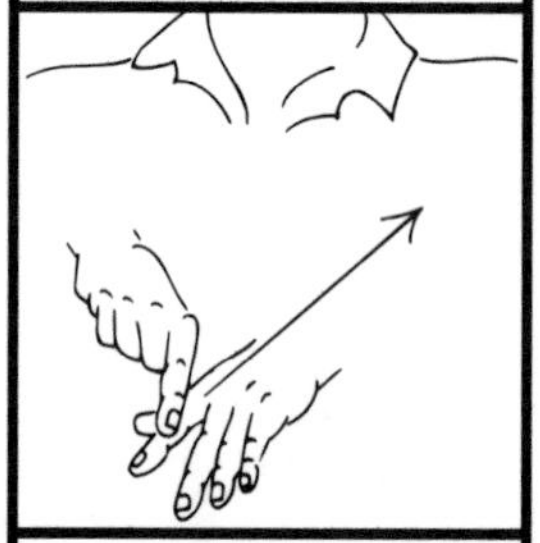
A. Long
B. Tall
C. Come

12 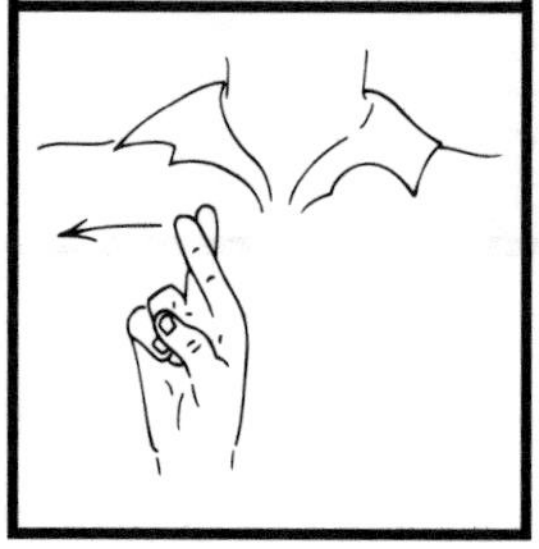
A. Resign
B. Right
C. Right Away

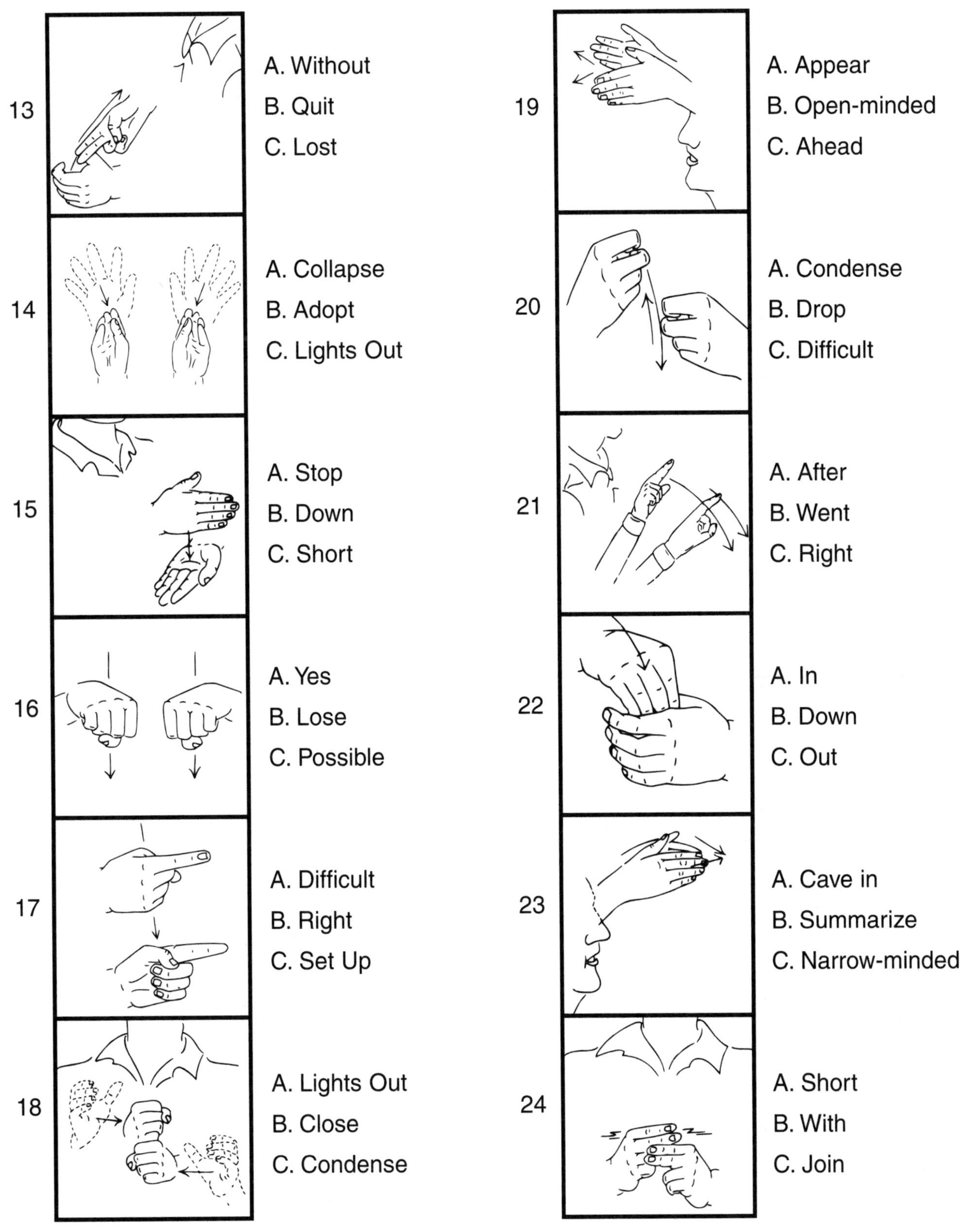

13
A. Without
B. Quit
C. Lost

14
A. Collapse
B. Adopt
C. Lights Out

15
A. Stop
B. Down
C. Short

16
A. Yes
B. Lose
C. Possible

17
A. Difficult
B. Right
C. Set Up

18
A. Lights Out
B. Close
C. Condense

19
A. Appear
B. Open-minded
C. Ahead

20
A. Condense
B. Drop
C. Difficult

21
A. After
B. Went
C. Right

22
A. In
B. Down
C. Out

23
A. Cave in
B. Summarize
C. Narrow-minded

24
A. Short
B. With
C. Join

Chapter 8

Across 1
5
8
9
10
11
12
14
16
18
20
21
25
27
29
30
34
35
36
Down
1
2
3
4
5
6
7
13
15
17
18
19
22
23
24
26
28
31
32
33

Opposites

On the previous page, write the meaning for each sign given. Then fill in the appropriate blanks in the crossword puzzle on this page.

1 2 3 4 5 6 7 8 9 10 11 12 13 14 15 16 17 18 19 20 21 22 23 24 25 26 27 28 29 30 31 32 33 34 35 36

Chapter 9

Location and Direction

Across

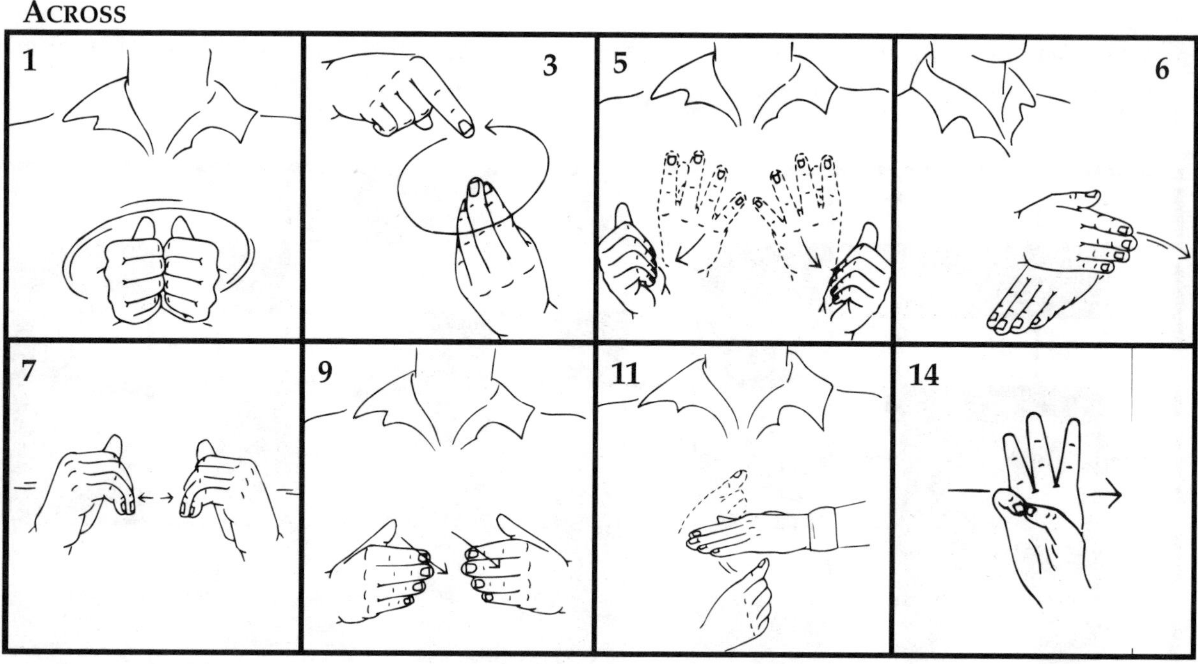

Down

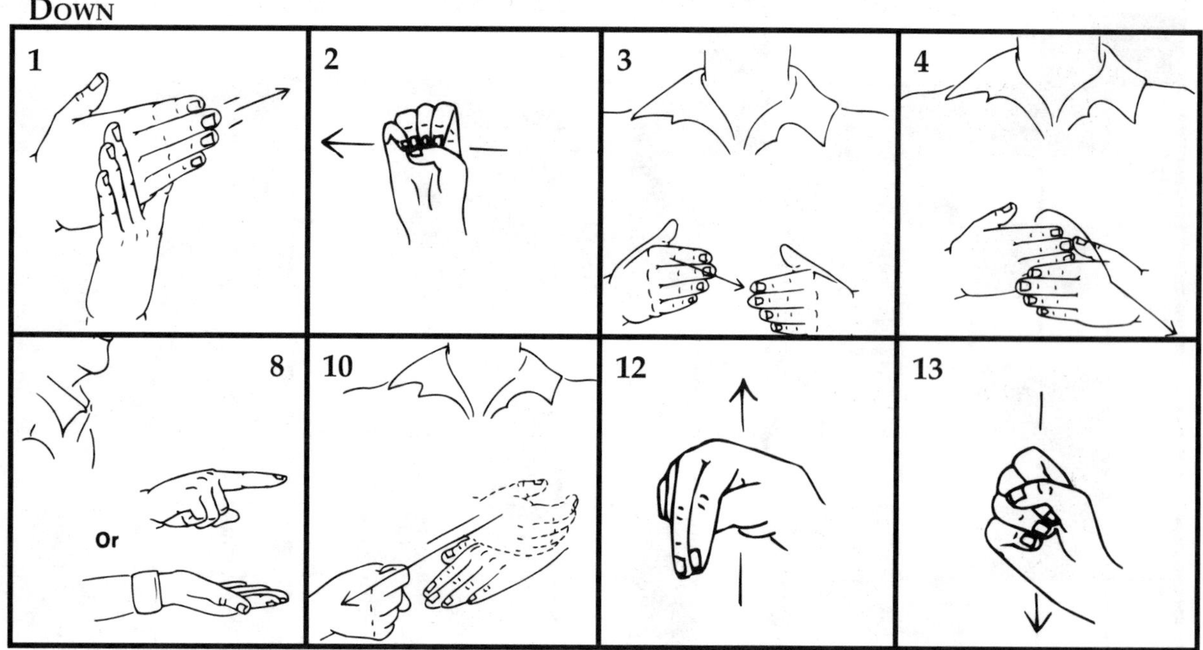

On the previous page, write the meaning for each sign given. Then fill in the appropriate blanks in the crossword puzzle on this page.

1 2 3 4 5 6 7 8 9 10 11 12 13 14

Chapter 9

Match the sign with its origin and the fingerspelled word. Write the number (sign) and the letter (origin) in the corresponding fingerspelled box.

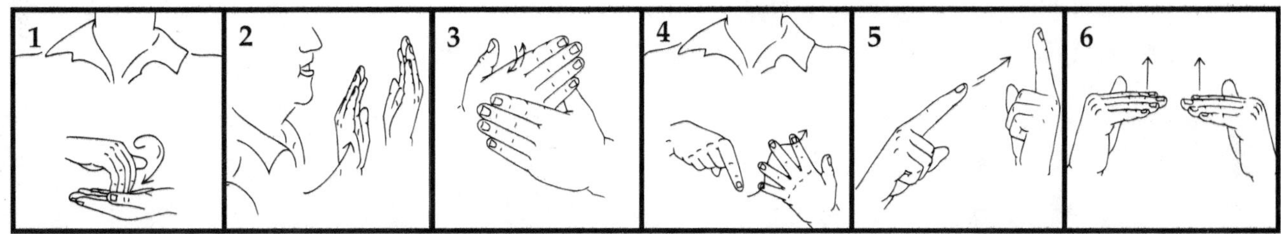

A.

B.

C.

D.

E.

F.

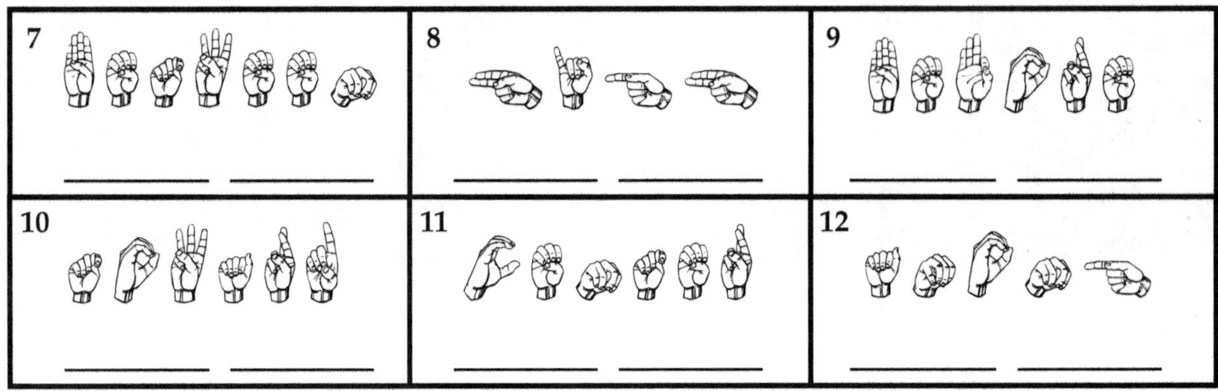

Chapter 10
Verbs and Related Words • Part 1

Spell the word for the sign given; write the letter below each hand position.

1 ___ ___ ___

2 ___ ___ ___ ___

3 ___ ___ ___

4 ___ ___ ___ ___

5 ___ ___ ___ ___

6 ___ ___ ___ ___

7 ___ ___ ___ ___

8 ___ ___ ___

9 ___ ___ ___ ___

10 ___ ___ ___

11 ___ ___ ___ ___

12 ___ ___ ___ ___

Chapter 10

ACROSS
1
3
5
7
10
11
13
14
15
16
19
20
23
24
25
27
30
31
33
34
DOWN
1
2
3
4
5
6
8
9
12
16
17
18
20
21
22
25
26
28
Or
29
32

Verbs and Related Words

On the previous page, write the meaning for each sign given. Then fill in the appropriate blanks in the crossword puzzle on this page.

Chapter 11

Verbs and Related Words • Part 2

ACROSS

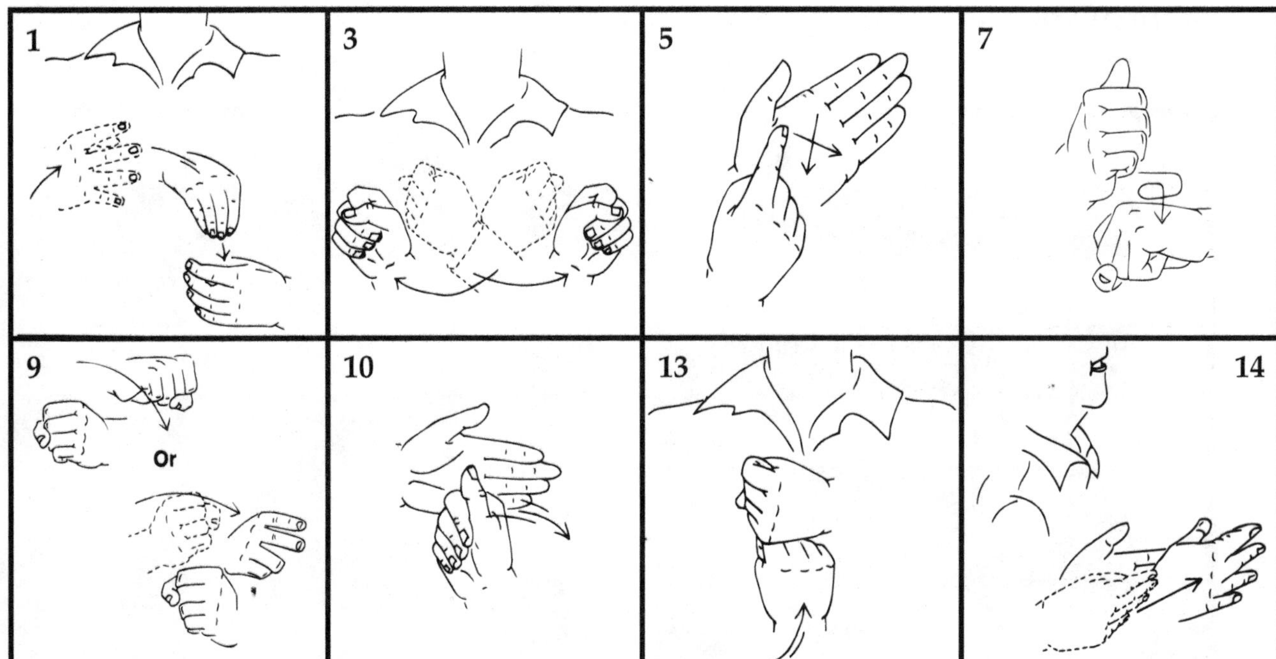

DOWN

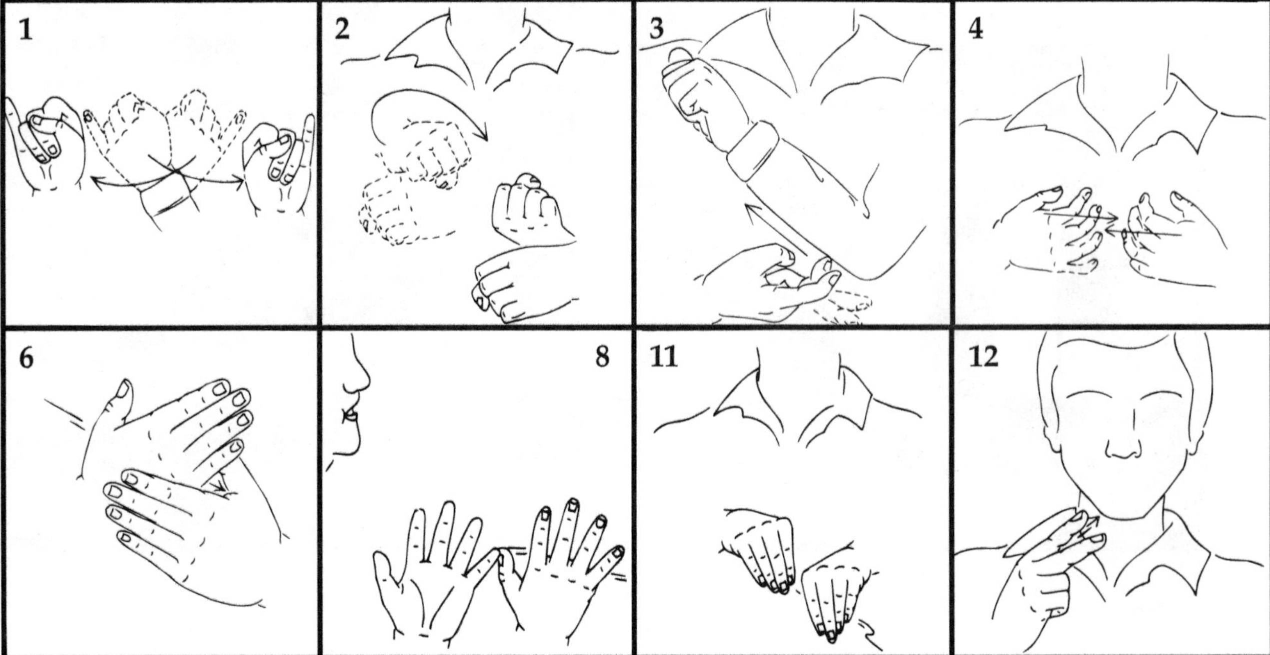

On the previous page, write the meaning for each sign given. Then fill in the appropriate blanks in the crossword puzzle on this page.

Chapter 11

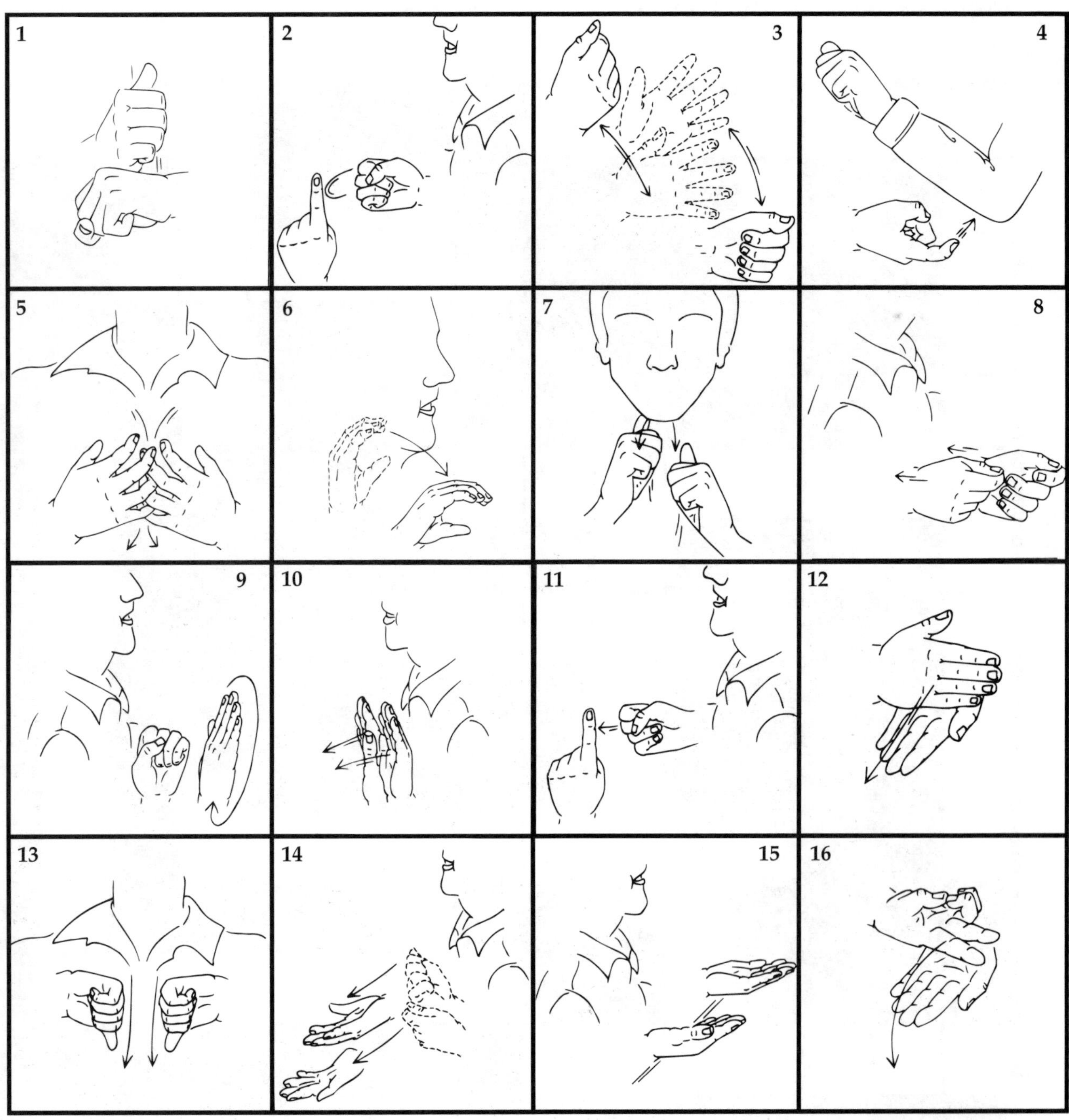

Verbs and Related Words

On the previous page, write the meaning for each sign. Then find the words in the seek-a-word puzzle. The words may read forward, backward, up, down, or diagonally.

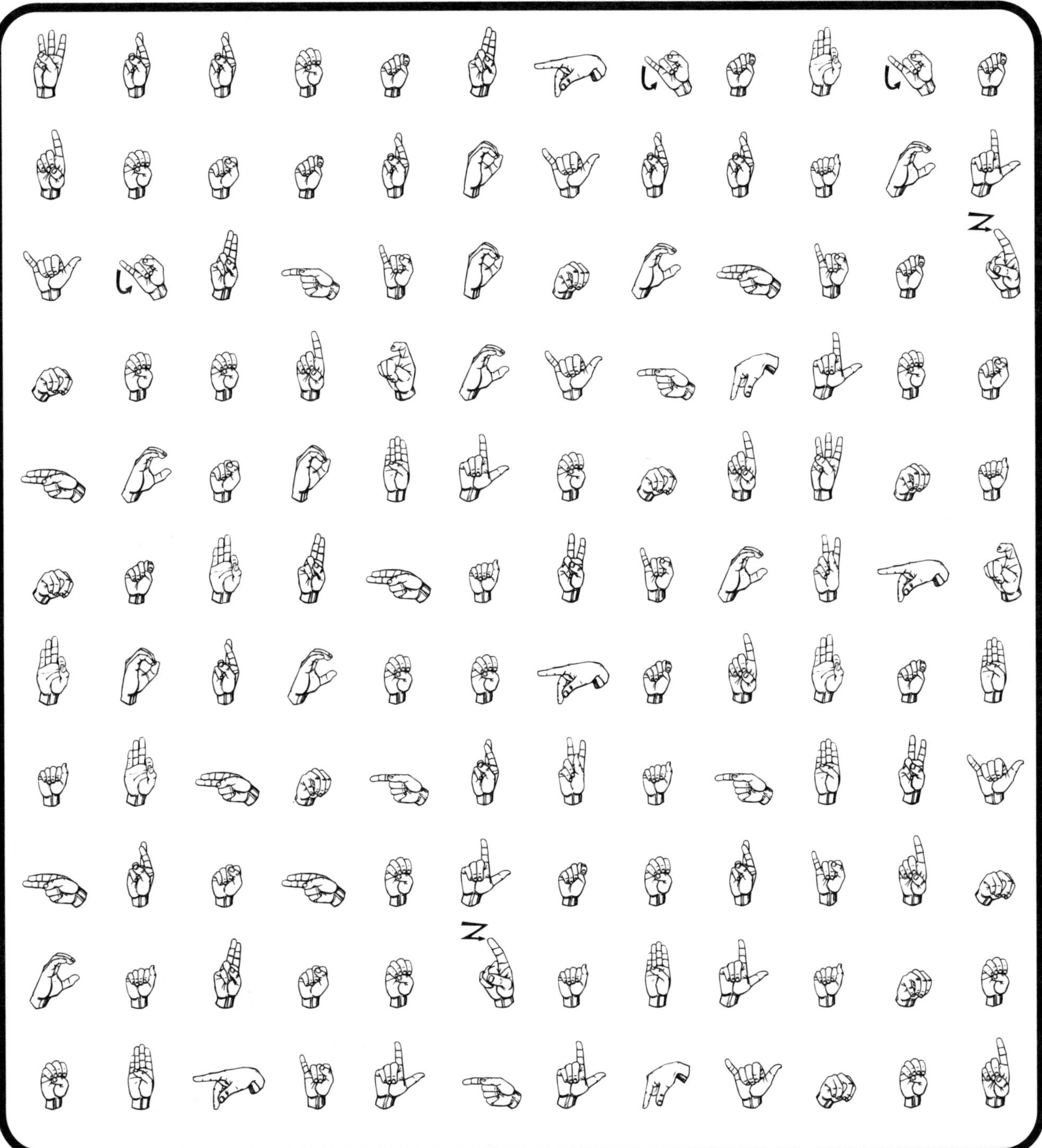

Chapter 12

Quality, Kind, and Condition

Underline the word that matches the given sign.

1 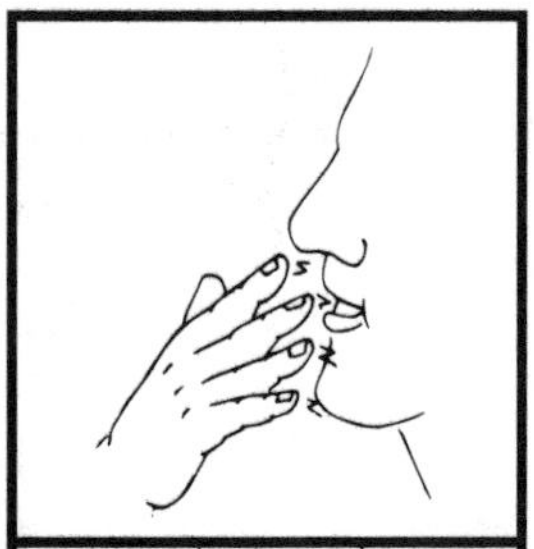
A. Color
B. Noisy
C. Warm

2 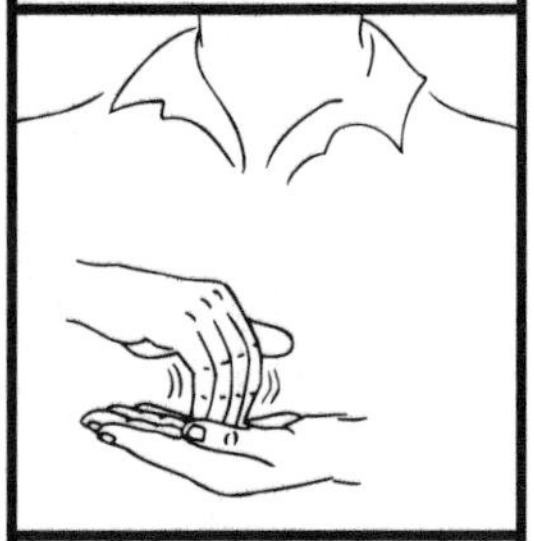
A. Medium
B. Smooth
C. Weak

3 
A. Confusion
B. Color
C. Odd

4 
A. Smooth
B. Fine
C. Sharp

5 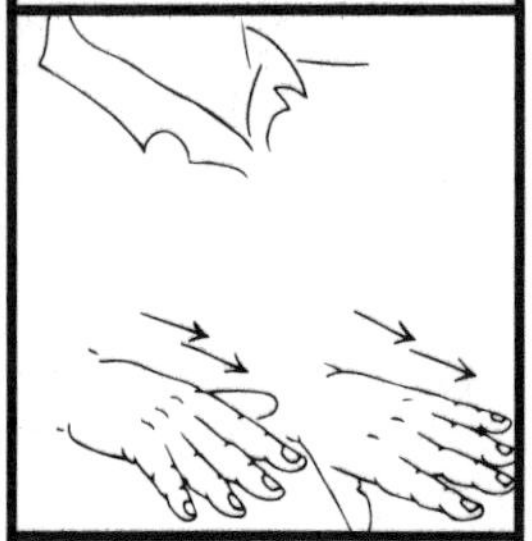
A. Vibration
B. Great
C. Calm

6 
A. Smooth
B. Shining
C. Sharp

7 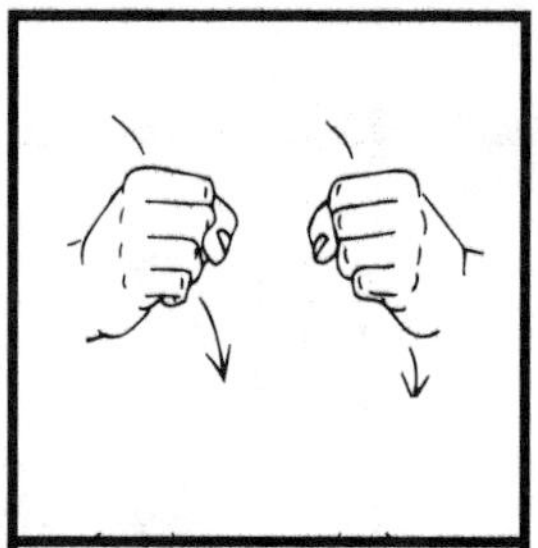
A. Danger
B. Cold
C. Strong

8 
A. Blue
B. Brown
C. Fine

9 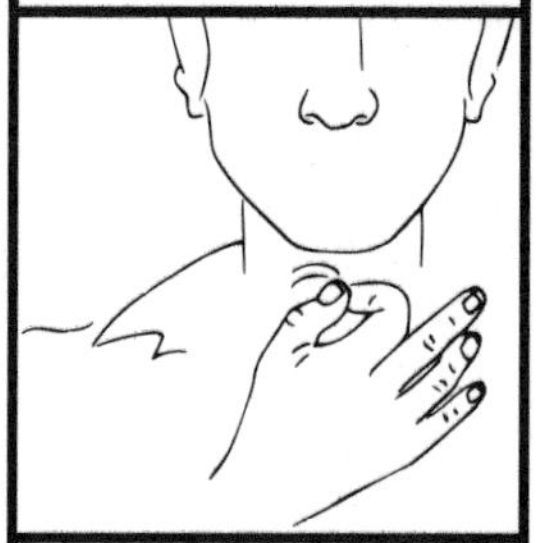
A. Favorite
B. Curious
C. Lucky

10 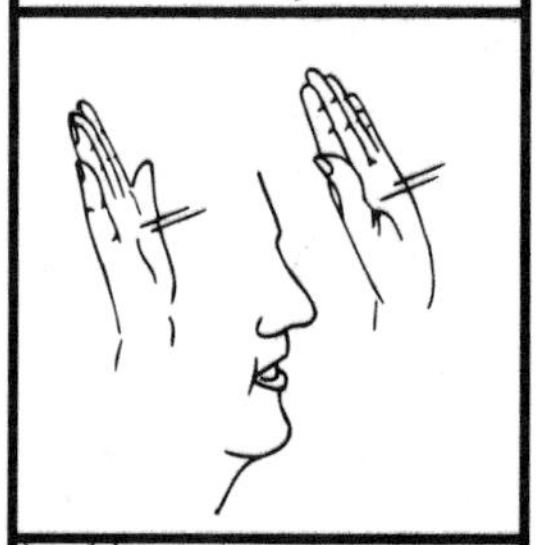
A. Wonderful
B. Pretty
C. Best

11 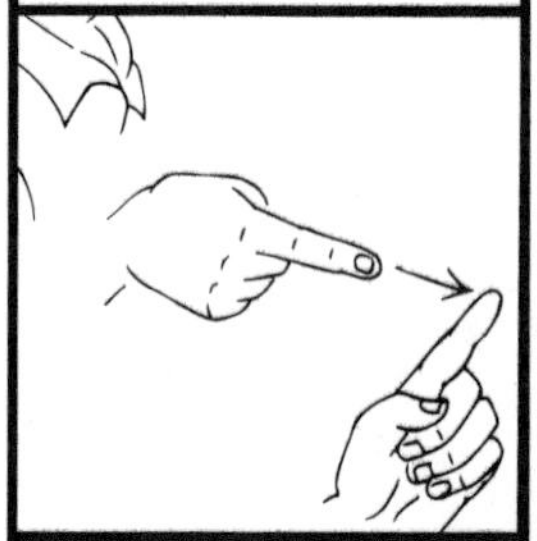
A. Same
B. Specific
C. Exact

12 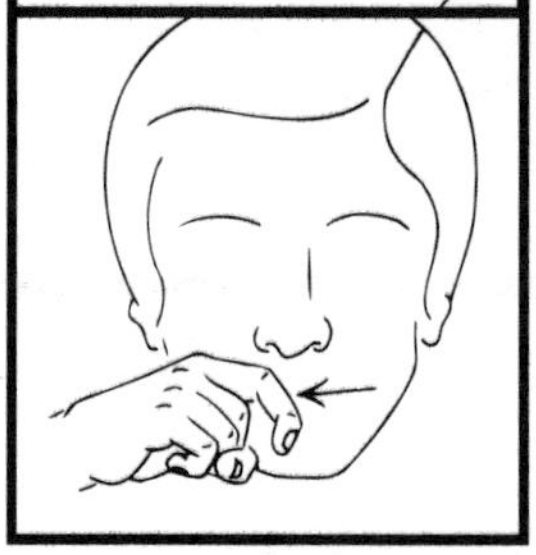
A. Red
B. Quiet
C. Dry

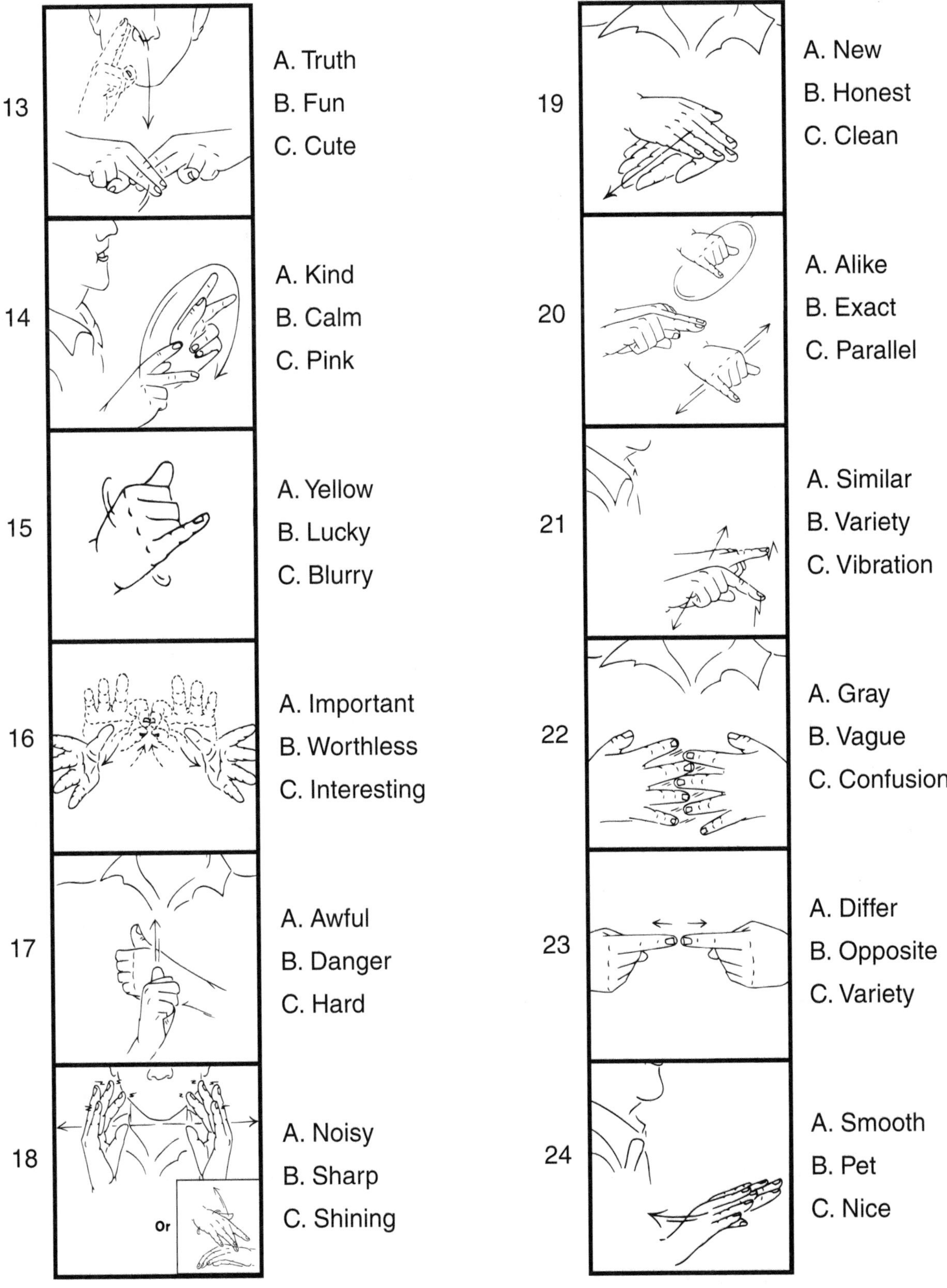

13
A. Truth
B. Fun
C. Cute

14
A. Kind
B. Calm
C. Pink

15
A. Yellow
B. Lucky
C. Blurry

16
A. Important
B. Worthless
C. Interesting

17
A. Awful
B. Danger
C. Hard

18
A. Noisy
B. Sharp
C. Shining

19
A. New
B. Honest
C. Clean

20
A. Alike
B. Exact
C. Parallel

21
A. Similar
B. Variety
C. Vibration

22
A. Gray
B. Vague
C. Confusion

23
A. Differ
B. Opposite
C. Variety

24
A. Smooth
B. Pet
C. Nice

Chapter 12

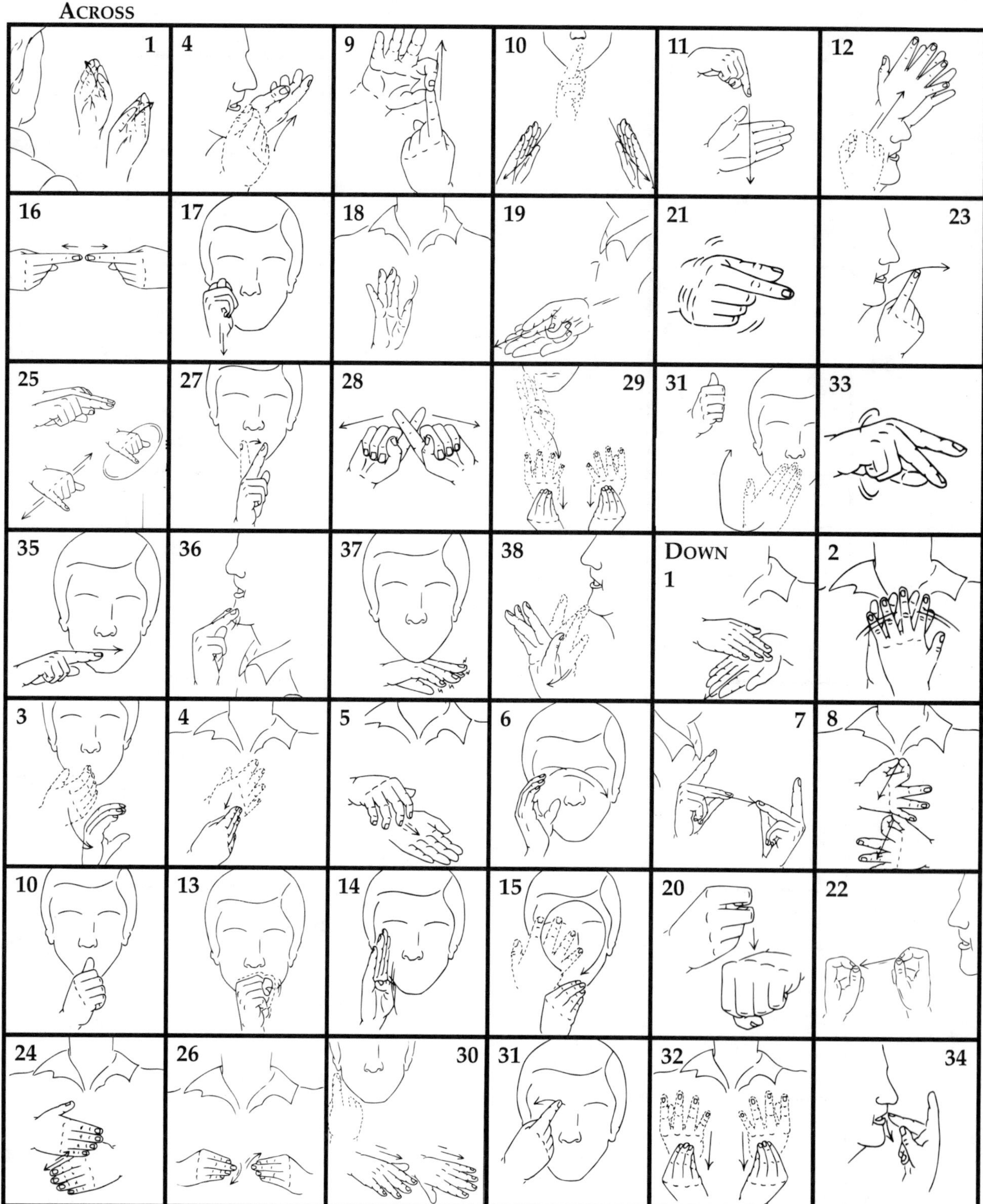
ACROSS
1
4
9
10
11
12
16
17
18
19
21
23
25
27
28
29
31
33
35
36
37
38
DOWN
1
2
3
4
5
6
7
8
10
13
14
15
20
22
24
26
30
31
32
34

Quality, Kind, and Condition

On the previous page, write the meaning for each sign given. Then fill in the appropriate blanks in the crossword puzzle on this page.

Chapter 13
Quantity, Size and Degree

Across

1	3	4	7
9	11	13 Or	14

Down

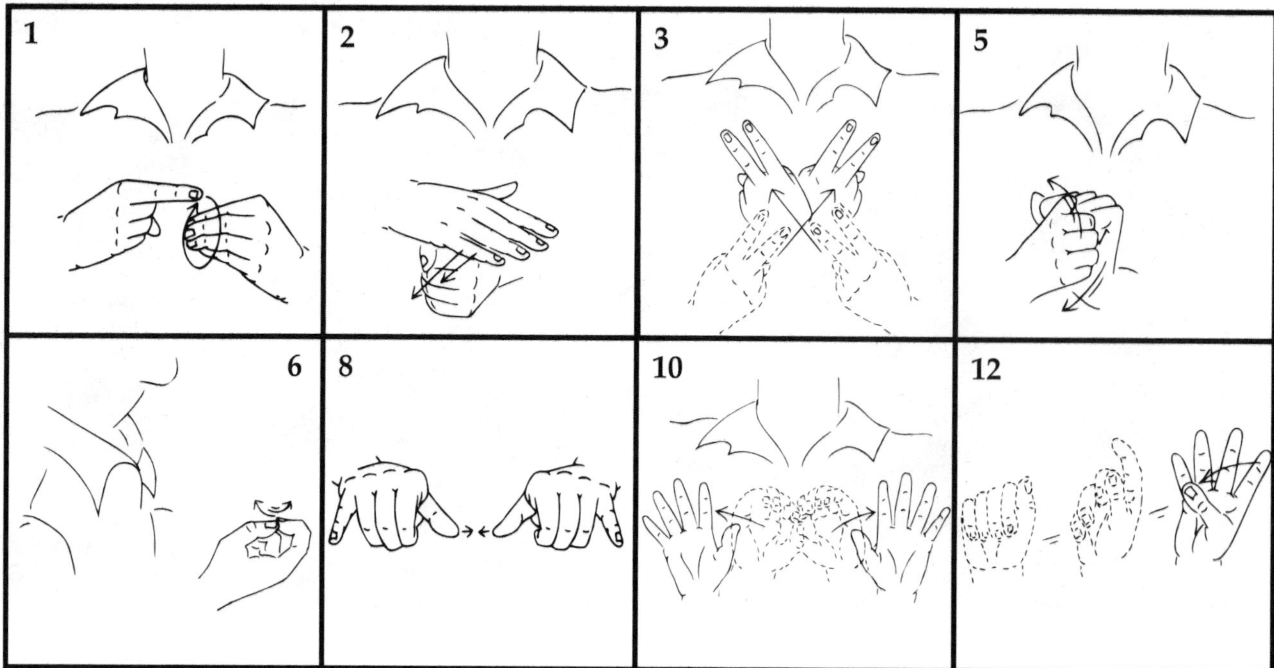

On the previous page, write the meaning for each sign given. Then fill in the appropriate blanks in the crossword puzzle on this page.

Chapter 13

Match the sign with its origin and the fingerspelled word. Write the number (sign) and the letter (origin) in the corresponding fingerspelled box.

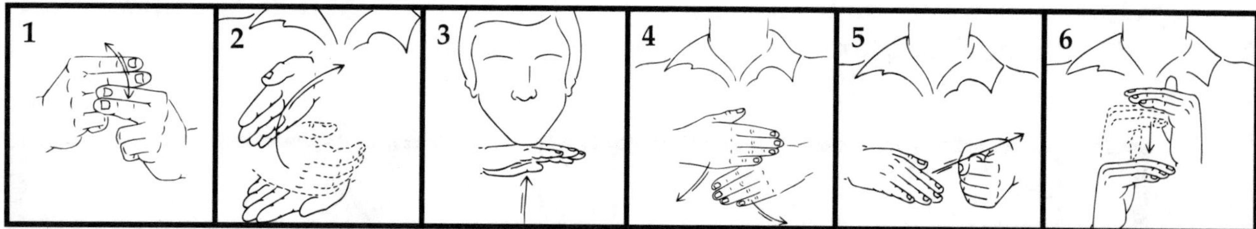

A.

B.

C.

D.

E.

F.

7 ______ ______	8 ______ ______	9 ______ ______
10 ______ ______	11 ______ ______	12 ______ ______

Chapter 14
Communication and Government

The fingerspelling for each sign is scrambled. Write the correct letter below each hand position, then unscramble the letters to form the correct word for each sign.

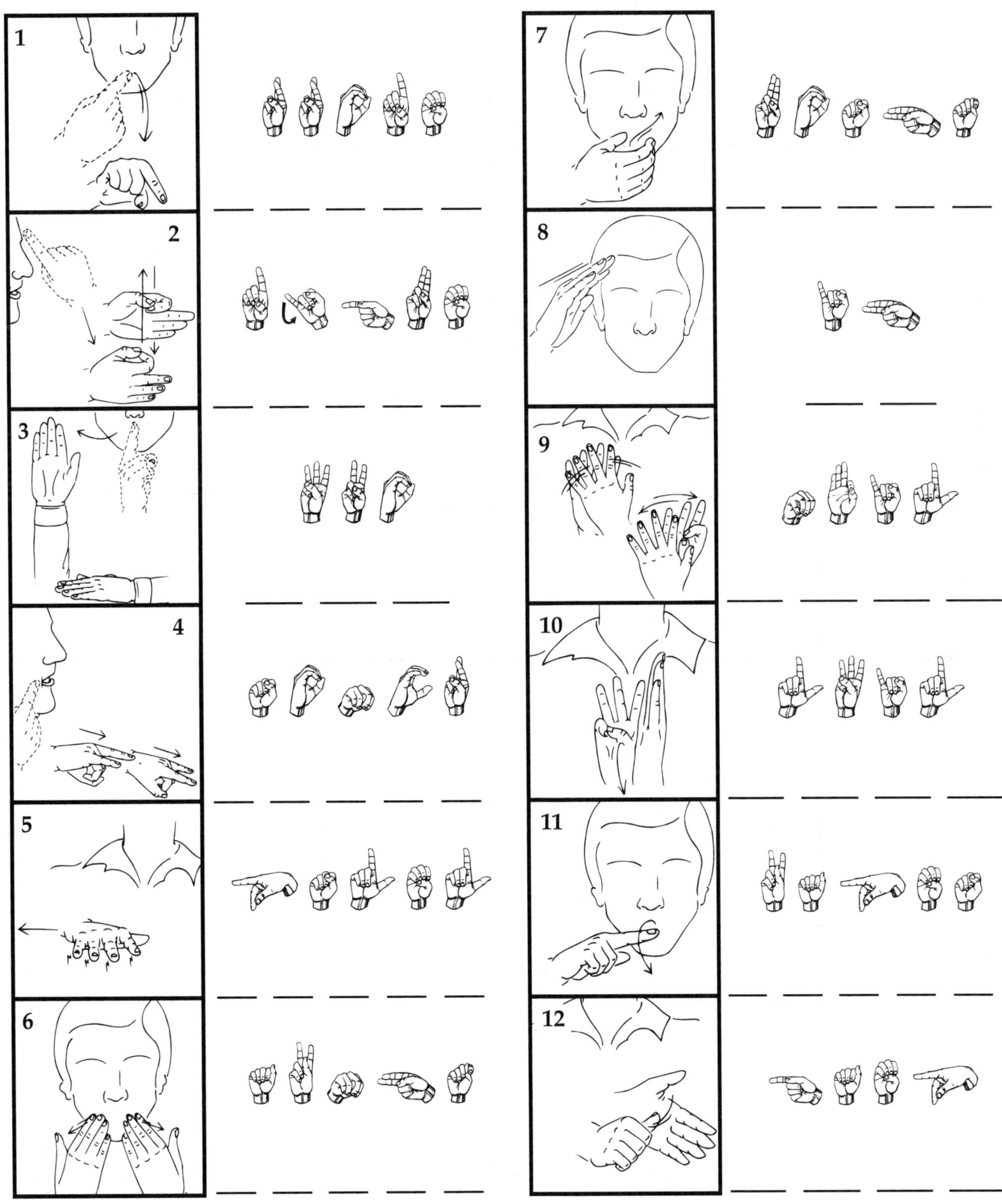

Chapter 14

ACROSS

Communication and Government

On the previous page, write the meaning for each sign given. Then fill in the appropriate blanks in the crossword puzzle on this page.

1 2 3 4 5 6 7 8 9 10 11 12 13 14 15 16 17 18 19 20 21 22 23 24 25 26 27 28 29 30 31 32 33 34

Chapter 15

Education

Find the fingerspelled word for each sign given. Circle it, write the letters of the word underneath it, and write the corresponding number.

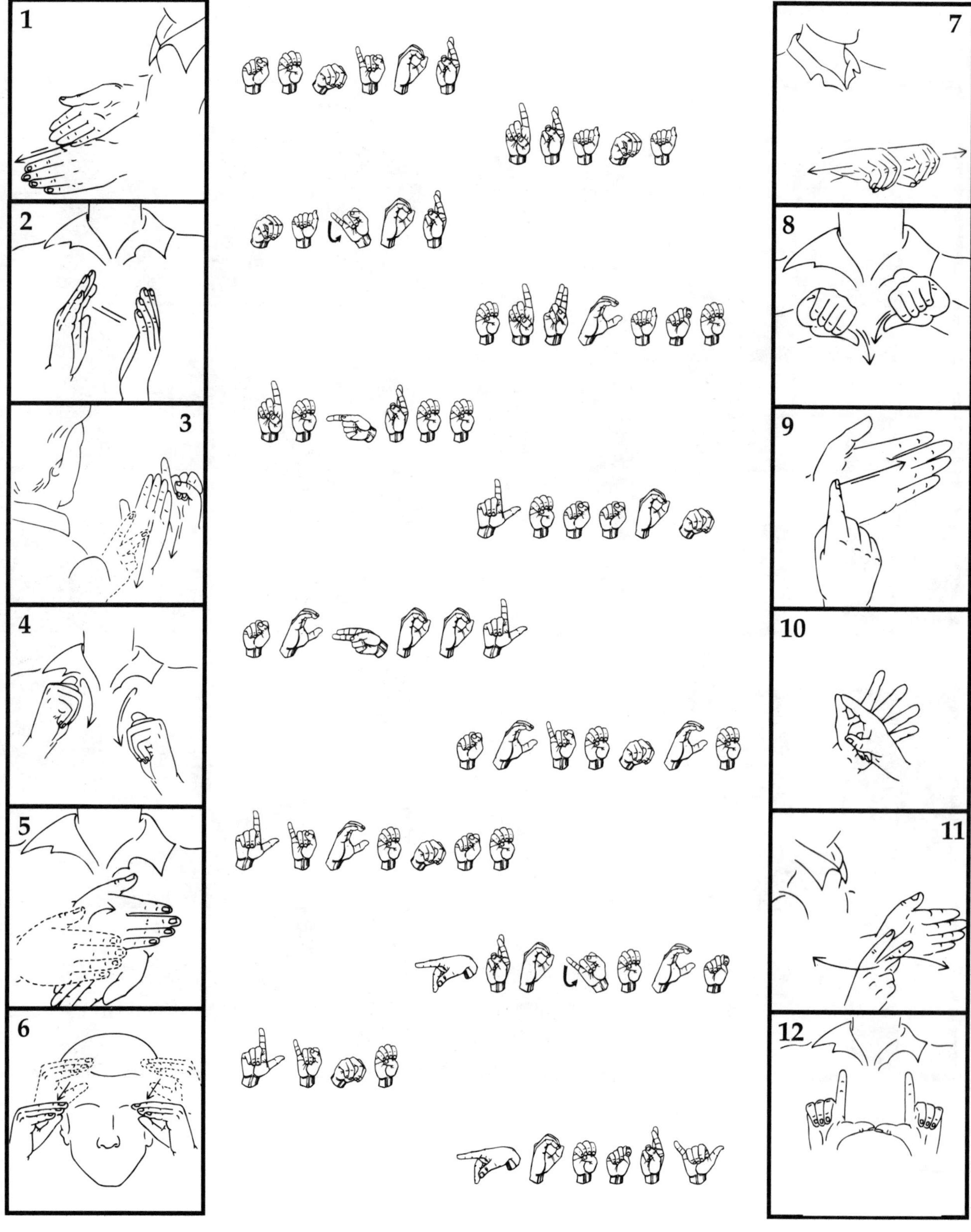

Match the sign with its origin and the fingerspelled word. Write the number (sign) and the letter (origin) in the corresponding fingerspelled box.

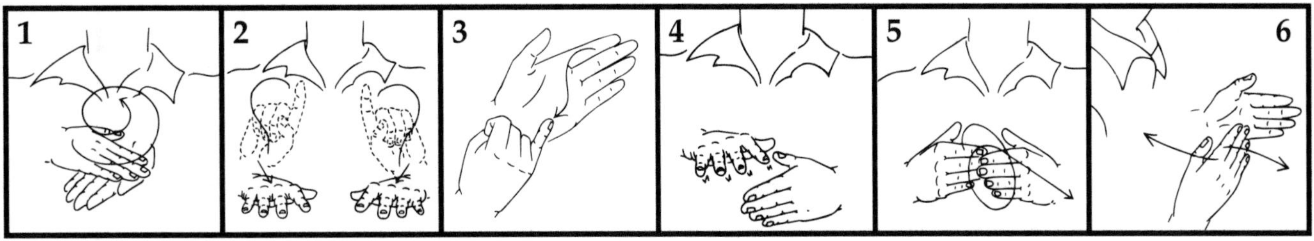

A.

B.

C.

D.

E.

F.

7	8	9
______ ______	______ ______	______ ______
10	11	12
______ ______	______ ______	______ ______

Chapter 16
Miscellaneous Nouns

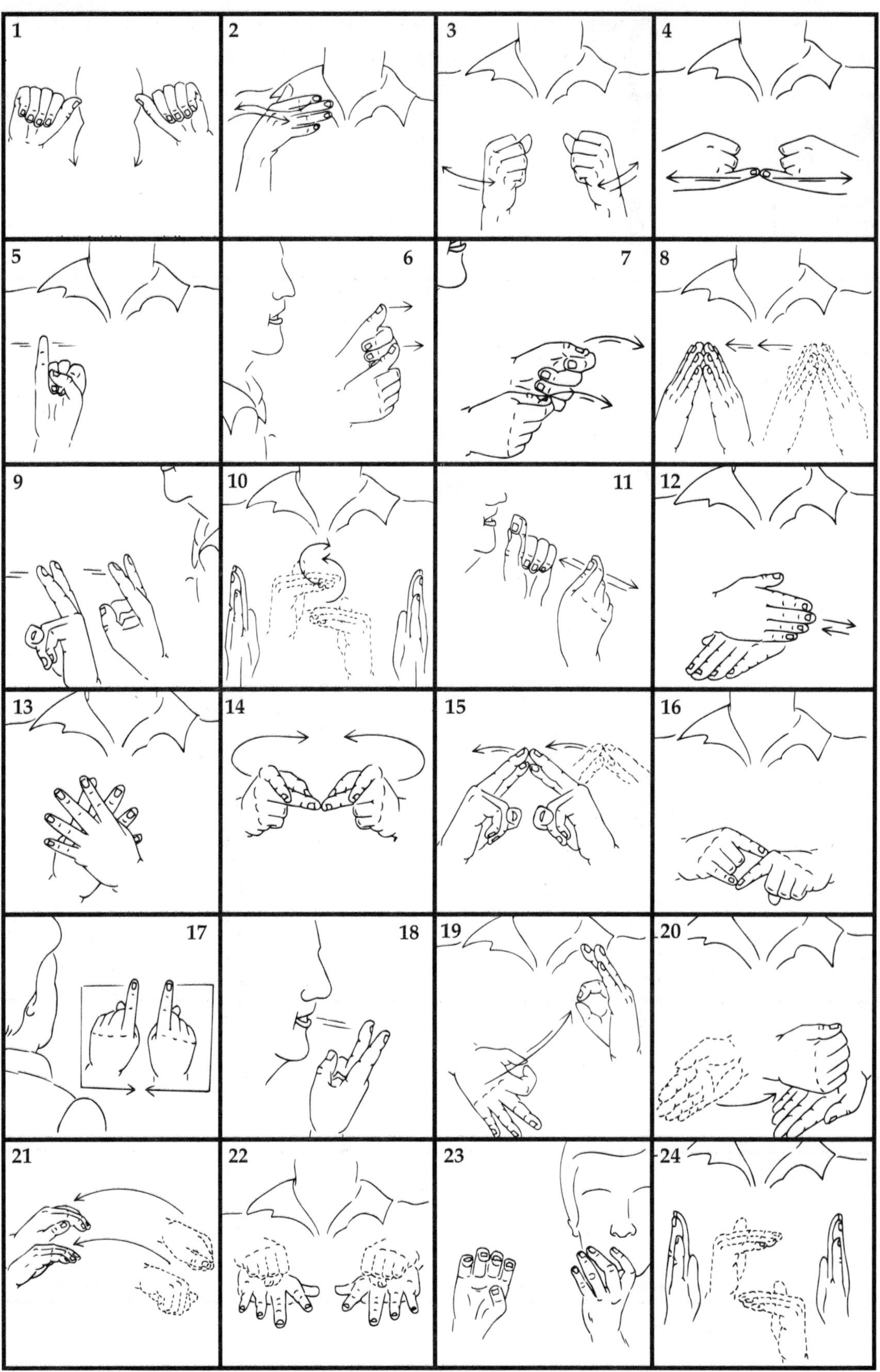

On the previous page, write the meaning for each sign. Then find the words in the seek-a-word puzzle. The words may read forward, backward, up, down, or diagonally.

B	W	A	S	L	I	D	A	E	R	H	T	X	H	F
J	P	I	P	M	A	Z	J	Y	O	W	F	P	G	L
Q	R	E	B	N	O	I	T	C	E	L	L	O	C	A
H	E	C	N	D	T	K	V	C	E	E	Y	S	K	G
R	S	N	B	O	X	N	I	V	P	O	S	T	E	R
M	E	A	K	G	B	C	M	N	O	P	L	I	A	J
A	N	R	H	C	A	M	P	U	G	L	G	N	L	A
G	T	U	S	J	E	X	O	M	A	A	L	G	T	U
I	Z	S	C	N	A	I	D	R	O	C	C	A	S	V
C	G	N	H	F	V	B	E	Z	T	E	S	N	I	I
B	U	I	L	D	I	N	G	N	A	N	E	O	B	L
I	A	W	B	I	U	D	W	F	K	Q	L	T	J	L
E	T	U	L	F	P	E	G	A	M	I	P	I	U	A
M	R	T	X	M	T	R	O	I	N	Q	Y	C	D	G
Y	F	C	P	C	I	G	A	R	E	T	T	E	G	E

Chapter 16

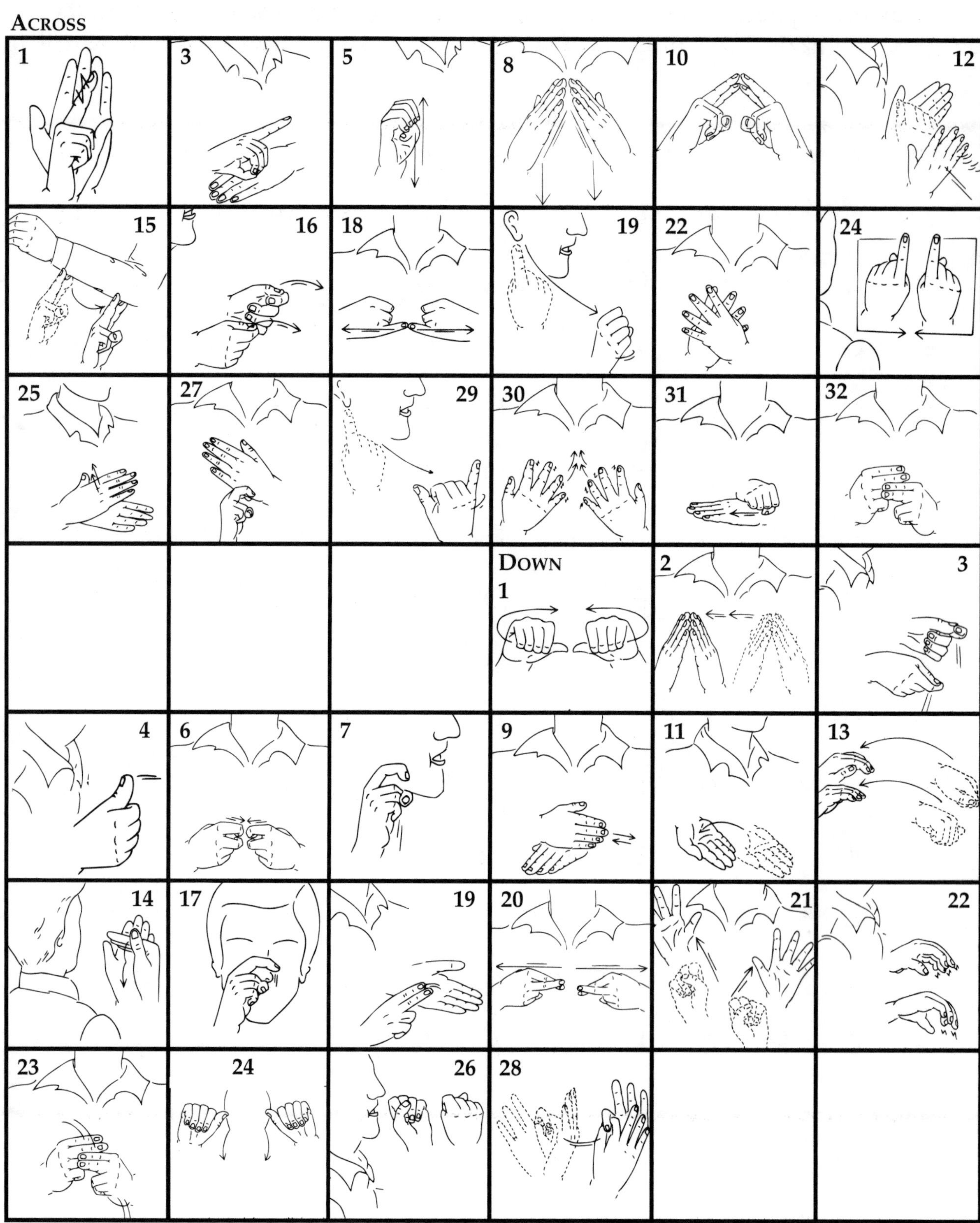
Across
1
3
5
8
10
12
15
16
18
19
22
24
25
27
29
30
31
32
Down
1
2
3
4
6
7
9
11
13
14
17
19
20
21
22
23
24
26
28

Miscellaneous Nouns

On the previous page, write the meaning for each sign given. Then fill in the appropriate blanks in the crossword puzzle on this page.

1 2 3 4 5 6 7 8 9 10 11 12 13 14 15 16 17 18 19 20 21 22 23 24 25 26 27 28 29 30 31 32

Chapter 17

Nature

The fingerspelling for each sign is scrambled. Write the correct letter below each hand position, then unscramble the letters to form the correct word for each sign.

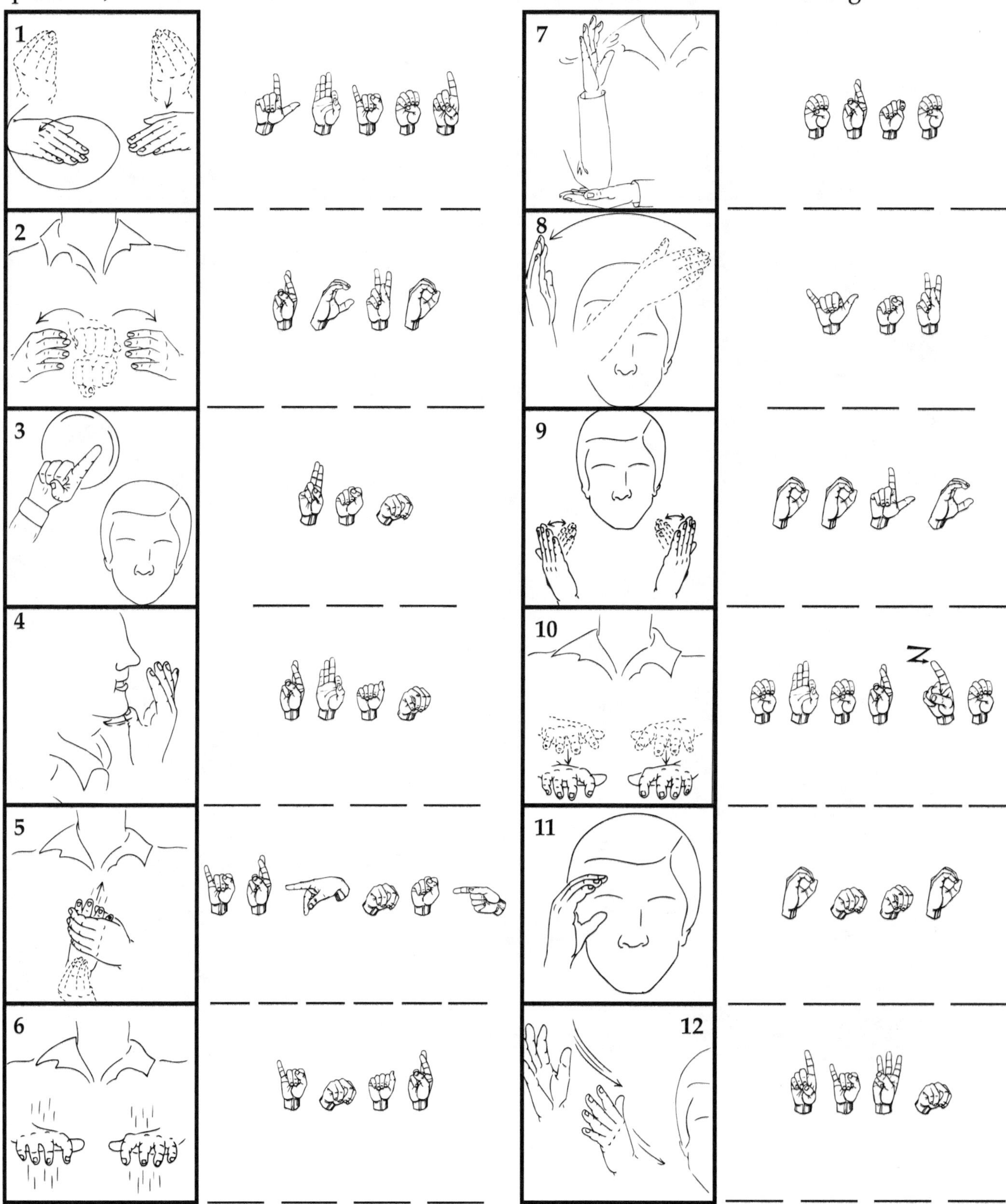

Match the sign with its origin and the fingerspelled word. Write the number (sign) and the letter (origin) in the corresponding fingerspelled box.

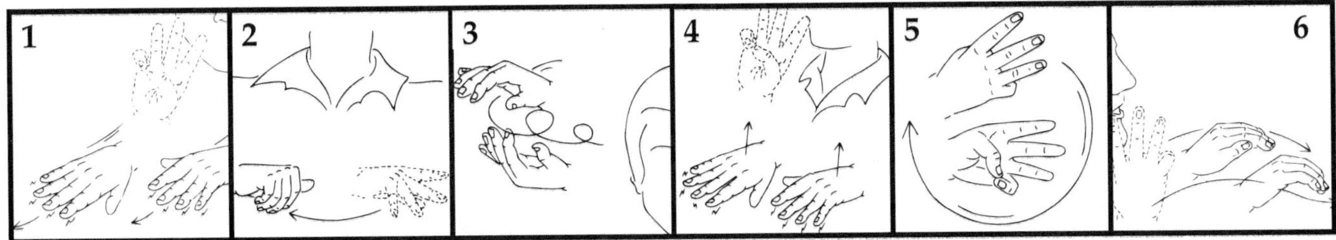

A.

B.

C.

D.

E.

F.

7	8	9
_______ _______	_______ _______	_______ _______
10	**11**	**12**
_______ _______	_______ _______	_______ _______

Chapter 18
Body, Health, and Medicine

Across

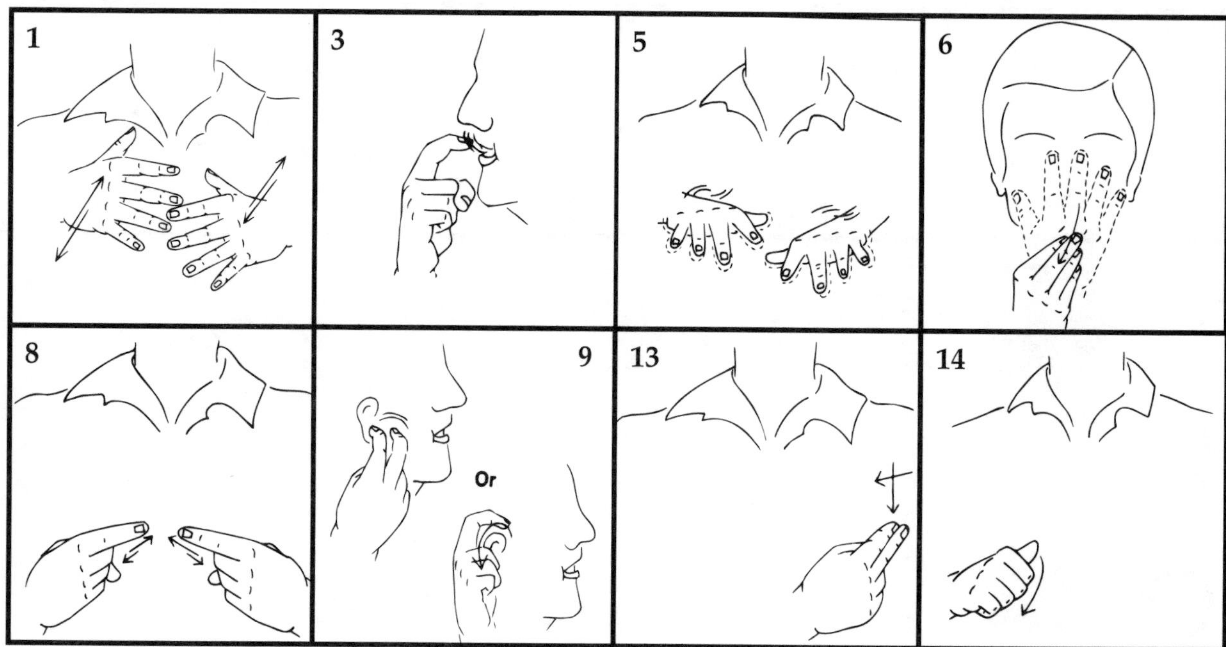

Down

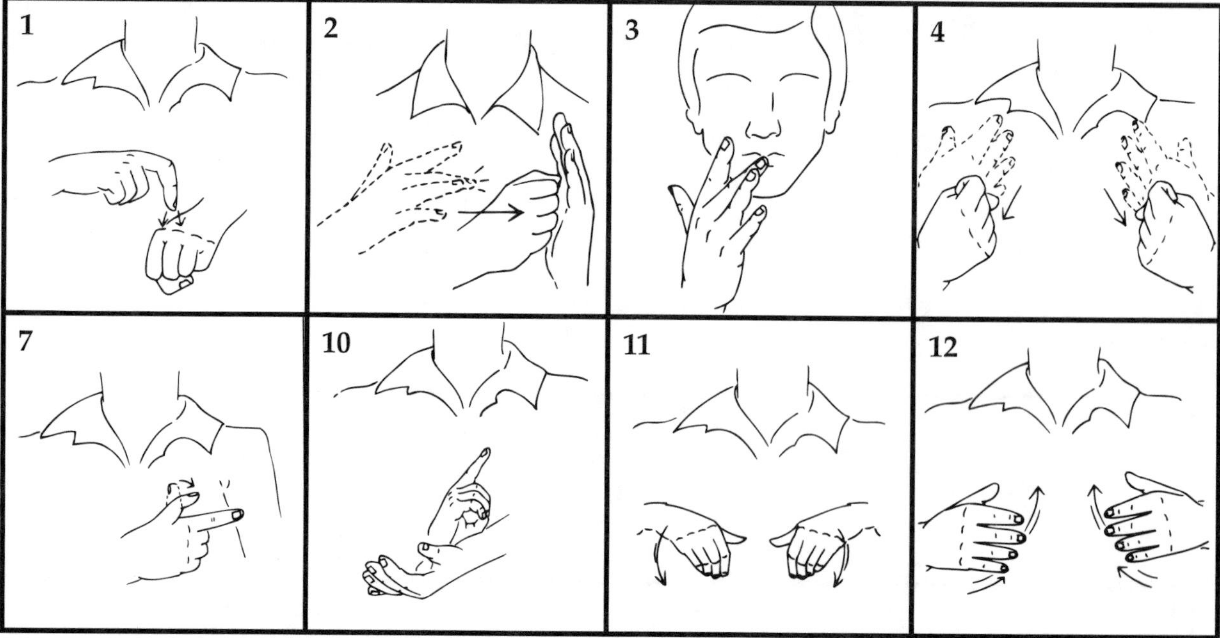

On the previous page, write the meaning for each sign given. Then fill in the appropriate blanks in the crossword puzzle on this page.

Chapter 18

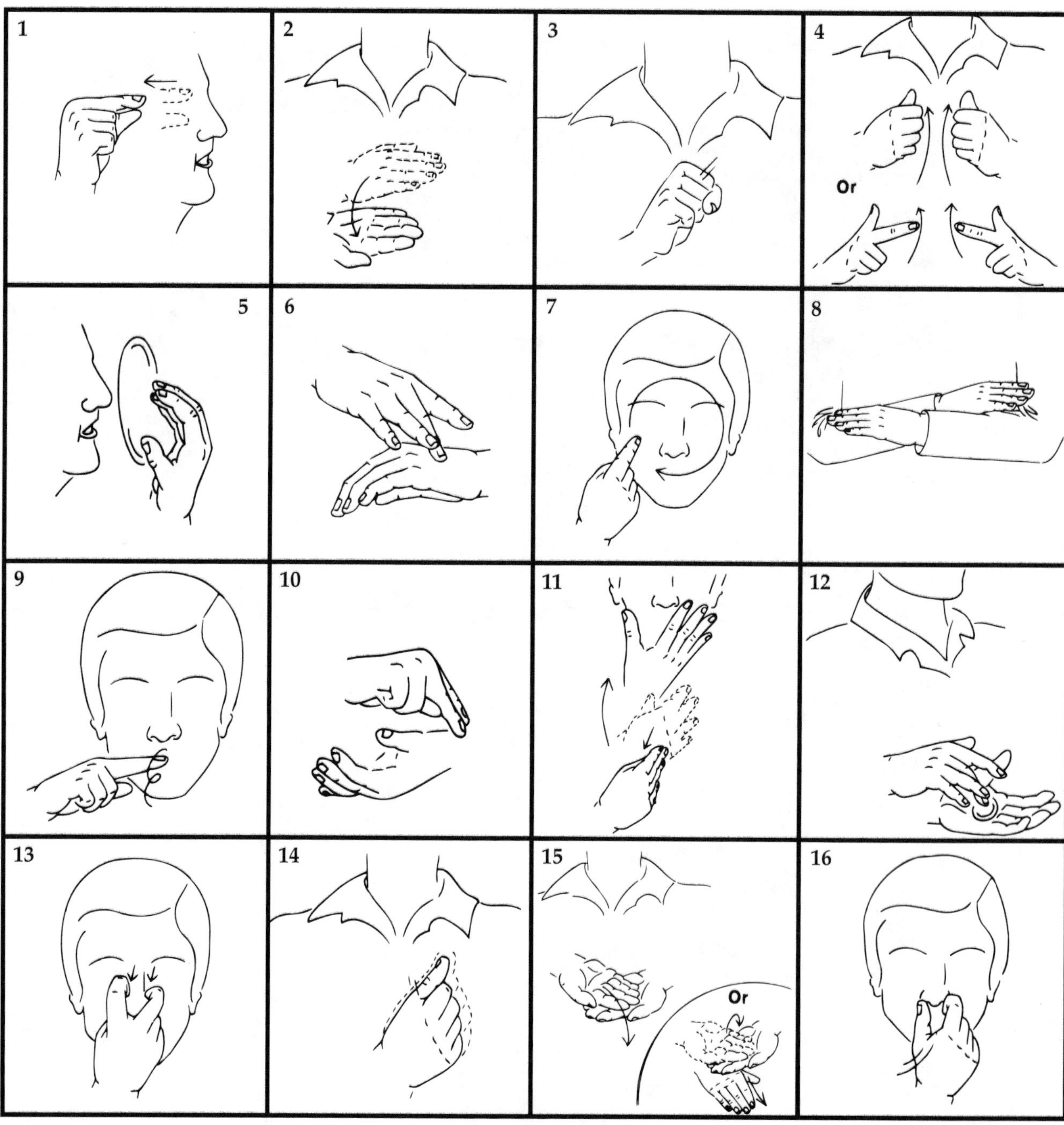

Body, Health, and Medicine

On the previous page, write the meaning for each sign. Then find the words in the seek-a-word puzzle. The words may read forward, backward, up, down, or diagonally.

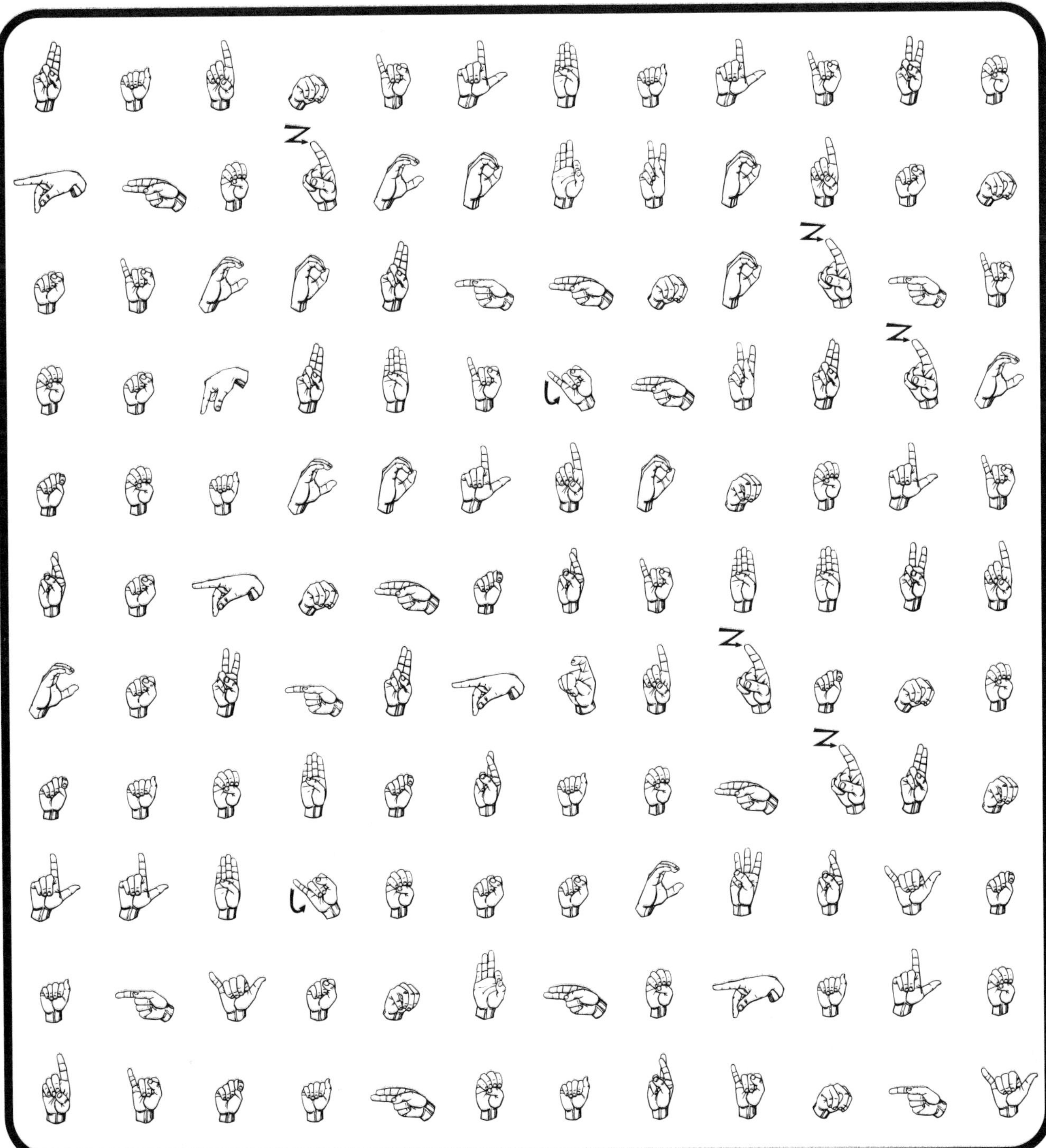

Chapter 19
Home, Furniture, and Clothing

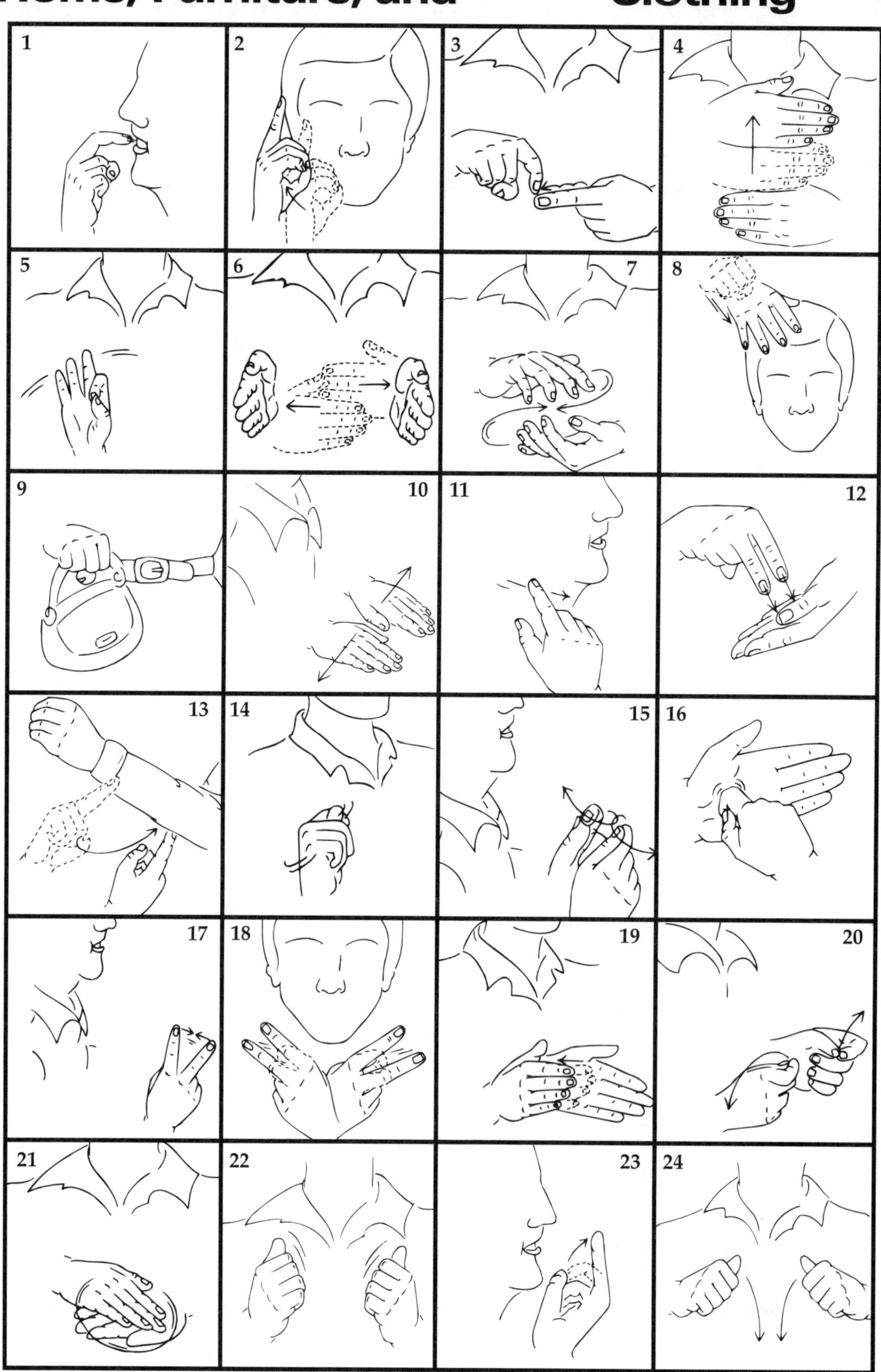

On the previous page, write the meaning for each sign. Then find the words in the seek-a-word puzzle. The words may read forward, backward, up, down, or diagonally.

E	B	R	E	C	A	C	S	T	Y	T	W	R	I	P
I	W	E	O	I	R	D	O	R	M	I	T	O	R	Y
T	F	A	R	O	D	Q	A	H	G	E	B	O	E	N
W	T	S	S	F	L	Z	P	U	F	X	A	M	L	T
O	H	M	D	H	A	F	U	R	N	I	T	U	R	E
B	O	A	J	C	I	X	T	B	E	T	F	O	R	K
Y	M	L	H	V	G	N	K	E	S	W	M	D	A	S
C	O	L	L	A	R	P	G	L	L	L	O	K	G	A
H	S	L	N	V	I	R	H	M	C	I	N	H	W	B
I	W	I	N	D	O	W	Q	Z	A	P	O	K	S	U
N	Q	G	I	W	P	I	Y	J	E	C	U	T	M	Y
A	T	H	J	U	S	E	H	S	I	D	H	S	A	W
D	S	T	R	U	K	X	L	L	F	Z	B	I	M	O
N	O	S	E	W	I	N	G	M	A	C	H	I	N	E
T	E	V	G	V	R	C	P	O	B	A	T	H	P	E

Chapter 19

Across

Home, Furniture, and Clothing

On the previous page, write the meaning for each sign given. Then fill in the appropriate blanks in the crossword puzzle on this page.

1 2 3 4 5 6 7 8 9 10 11 12 13 14 15 16 17 18 19 20 21 22 23 24 25 26 27 28 29 30 31 32 33

Chapter 20
Food and Related Words

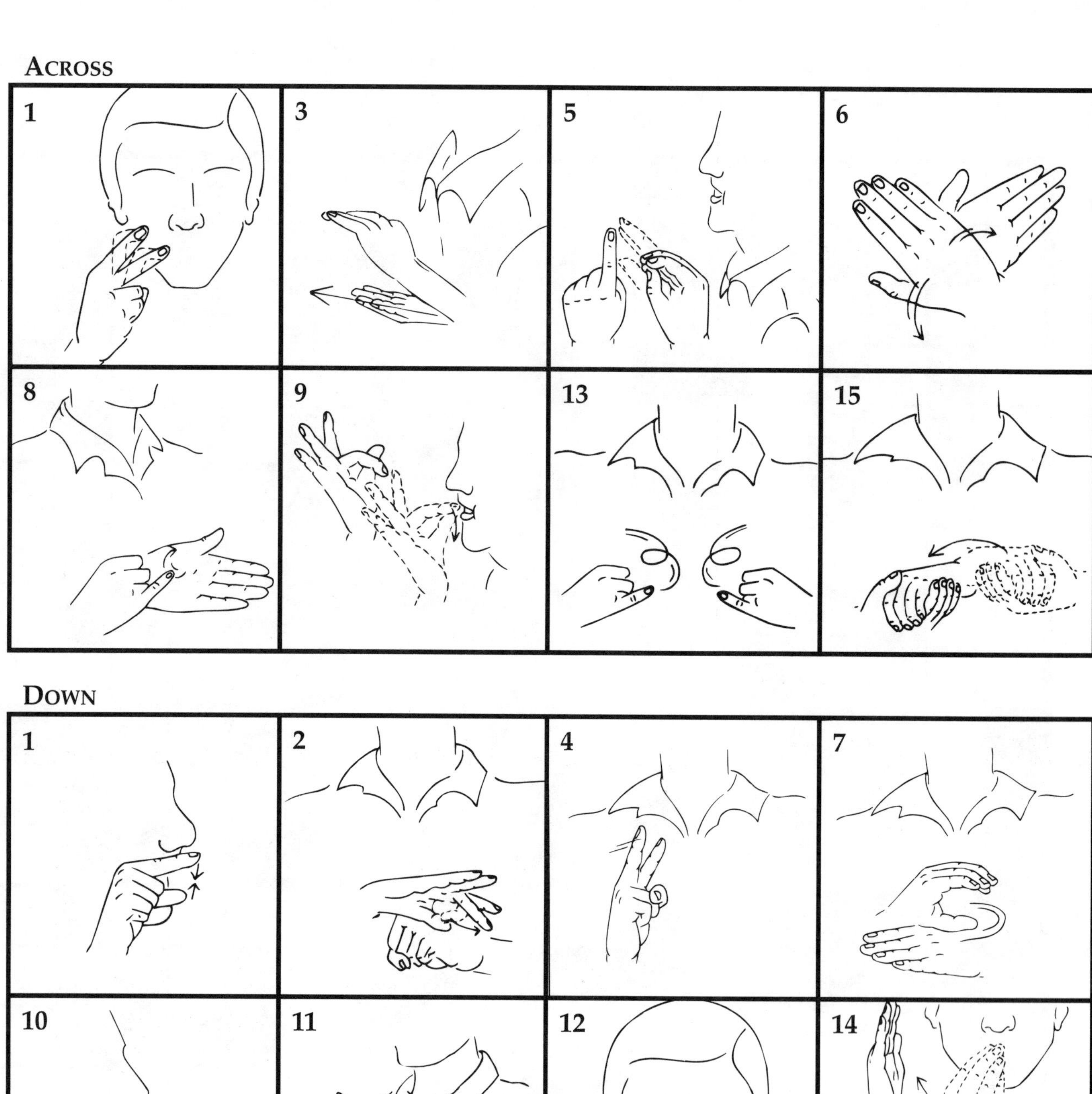

On the previous page, write the meaning for each sign given. Then fill in the appropriate blanks in the crossword puzzle on this page.

Chapter 20

ACROSS
1
3
8
9
10
12
13
15
17
19
20
23
24
26
27
28
33
34
35
36
37
DOWN
1
2
3
4
5
6
7
11
12
14
16
18
19
21
22
25
26
29
30
31
32

Food and Related Words

On the previous page, write the meaning for each sign given. Then fill in the appropriate blanks in the crossword puzzle on this page.

Chapter 21
Sports and Recreation

Find the fingerspelled word for each sign given. Circle it, write the letters of the word underneath it, and write the corresponding number.

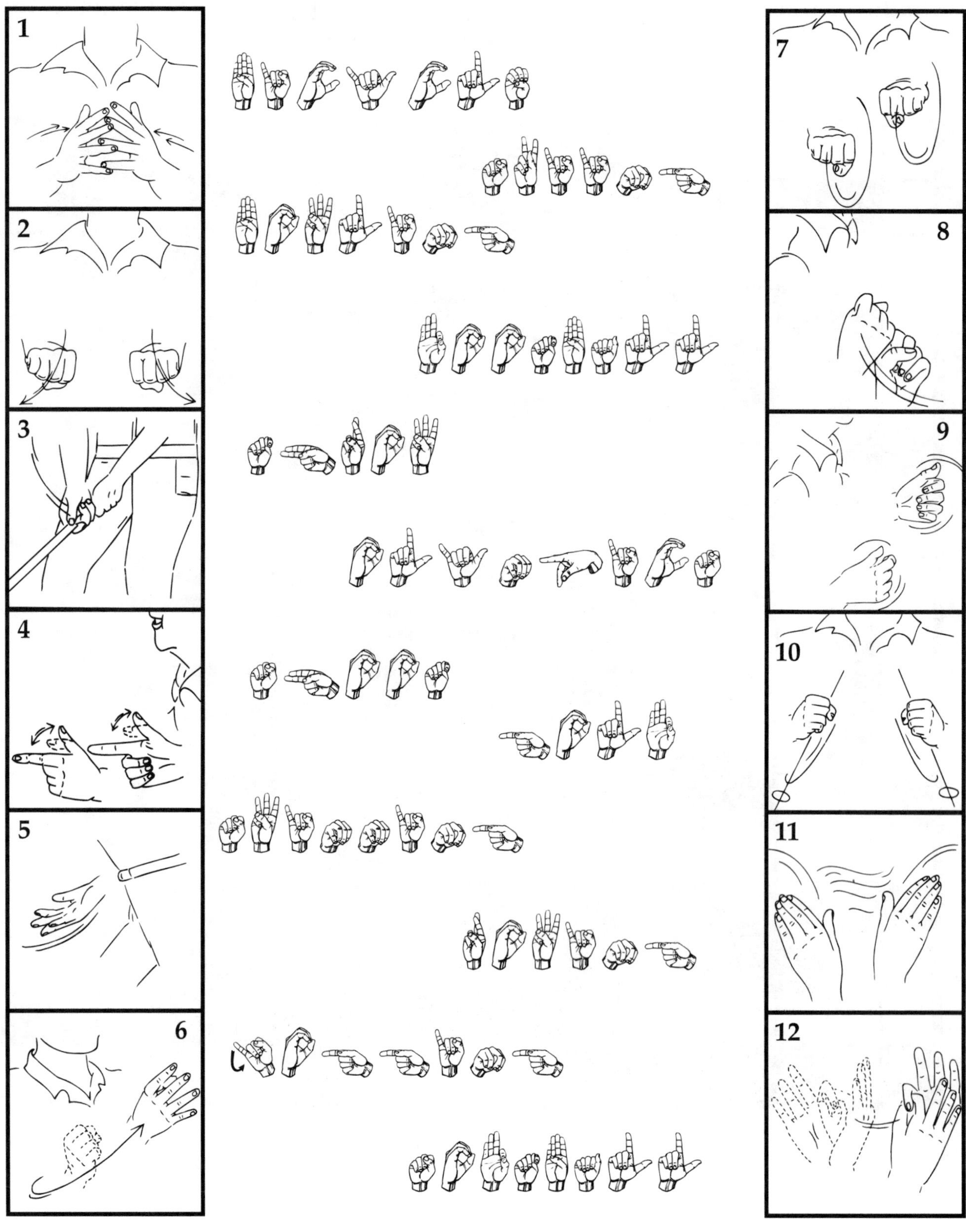

Match the sign with its origin and the fingerspelled word. Write the number (sign) and the letter (origin) in the corresponding fingerspelled box.

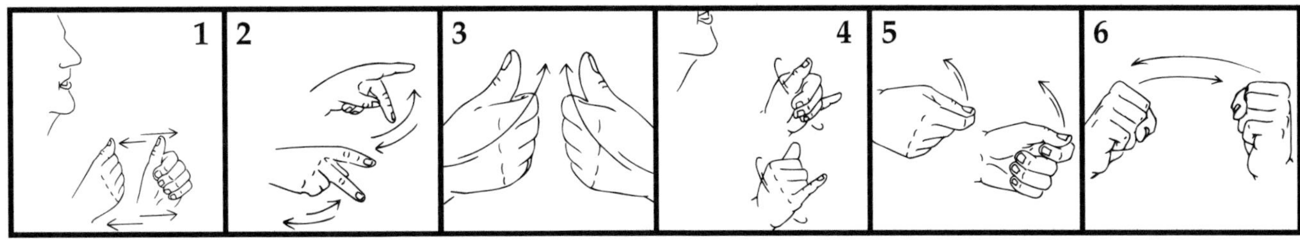

A.

B.

C.

D.

E.

F.

7	8	9
______ ______	______ ______	______ ______
10	**11**	**12**
______ ______	______ ______	______ ______

Chapter 22
Countries, Cities, and States

Underline the word that matches the given sign.

1 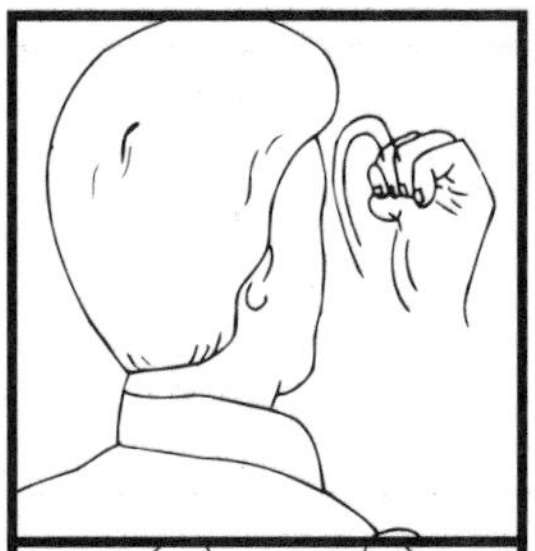
A. England
B. Europe
C. East

2 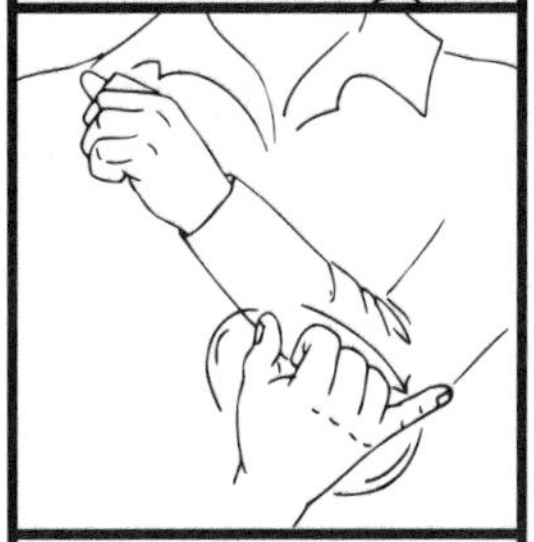
A. New York
B. Country
C. California

3 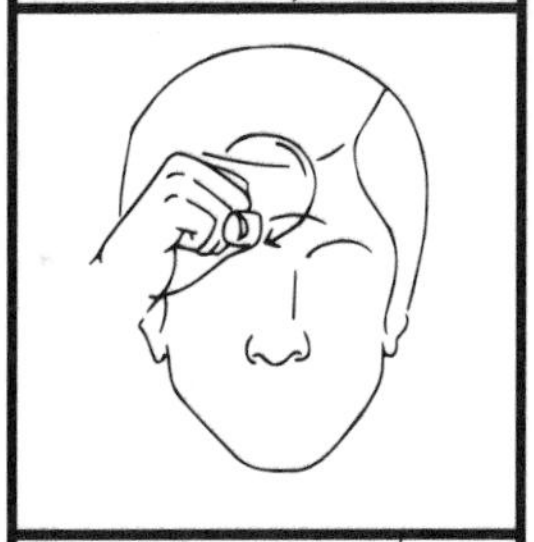
A. Sweden
B. Europe
C. State

4 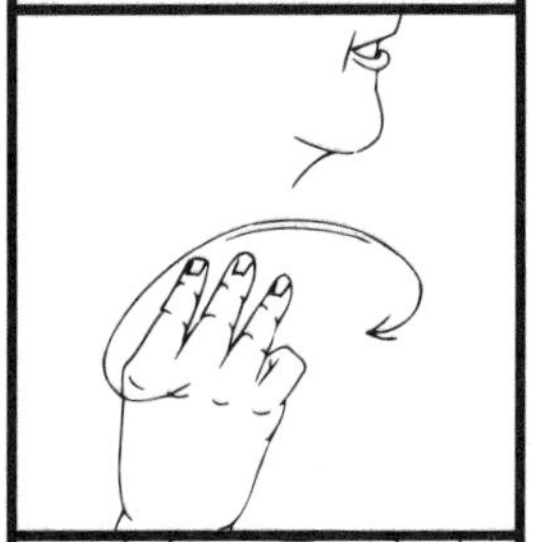
A. World
B. Chicago
C. Washington

5 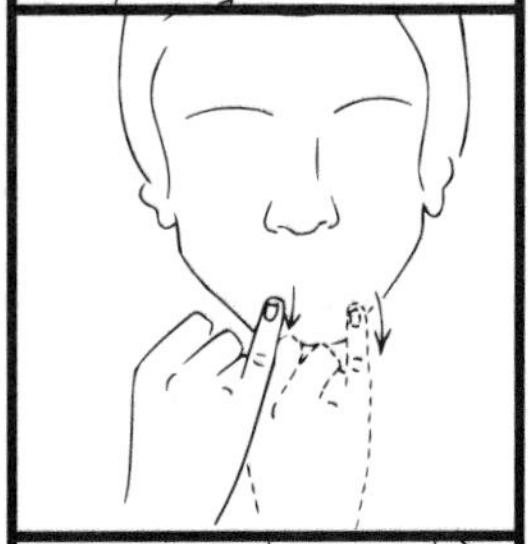
A. Dutch
B. Israel
C. Ireland

6 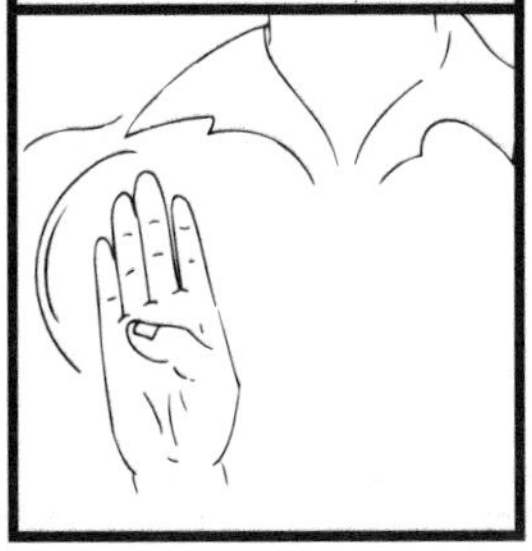
A. Denmark
B. Boston
C. France

7 
A. Spain
B. Nation
C. America

8 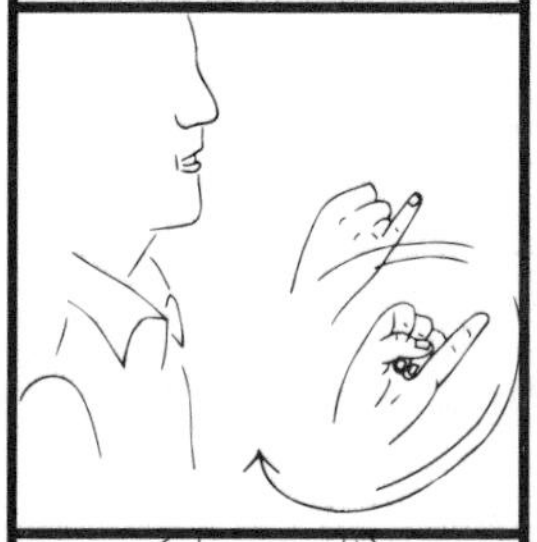
A. Ireland
B. International
C. Island

9 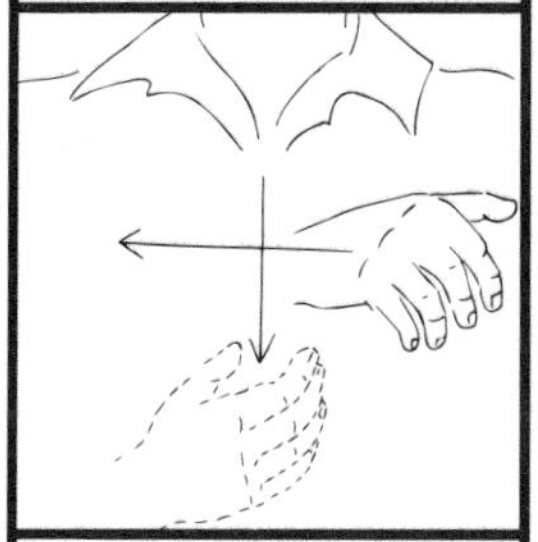
A. Scotland
B. Switzerland
C. Italy

10 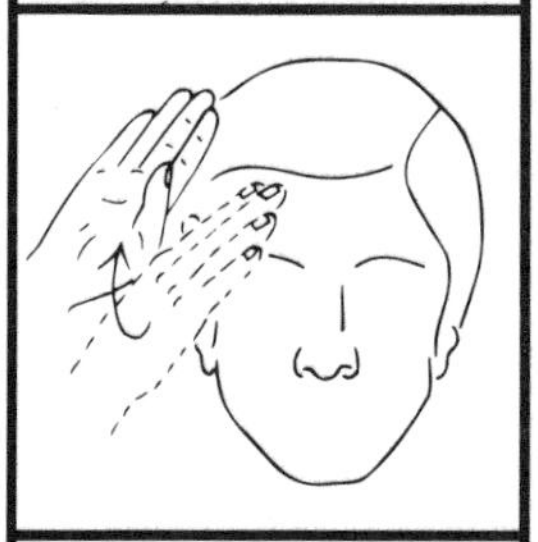
A. Canada
B. Germany
C. Australia

11 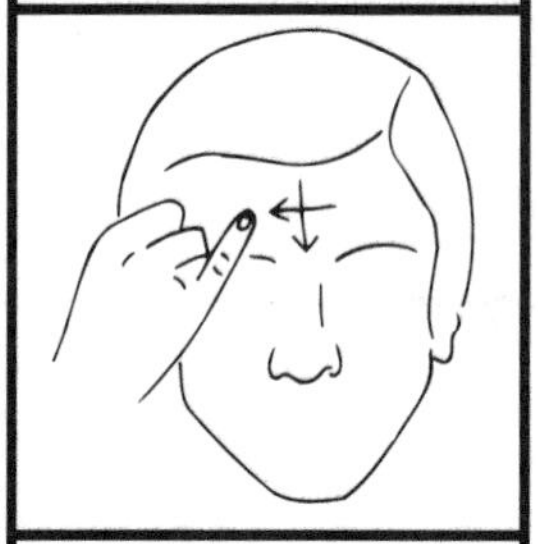
A. Italy
B. Roman
C. International

12 
A. Philippine Islands
B. Philadelphia
C. Pittsburgh

13
A. Russia
B. America
C. Germany

14
A. International
B. China
C. Korea

15
A. Holland
B. New York
C. California

16
A. Scotland
B. Canada
C. Boston

17
A. Nation
B. India
C. Norway

18
A. Foreign
B. New York
C. Country

19
A. Mexico
B. Minneapolis
C. Italy

20
A. Atlanta
B. America
C. Africa

21
A. California
B. Italy
C. Holland

22
A. Holland
B. Hawaii
C. Africa

23
A. America
B. World
C. Country

24
A. Detroit
B. Denmark
C. Minneapolis

Chapter 22

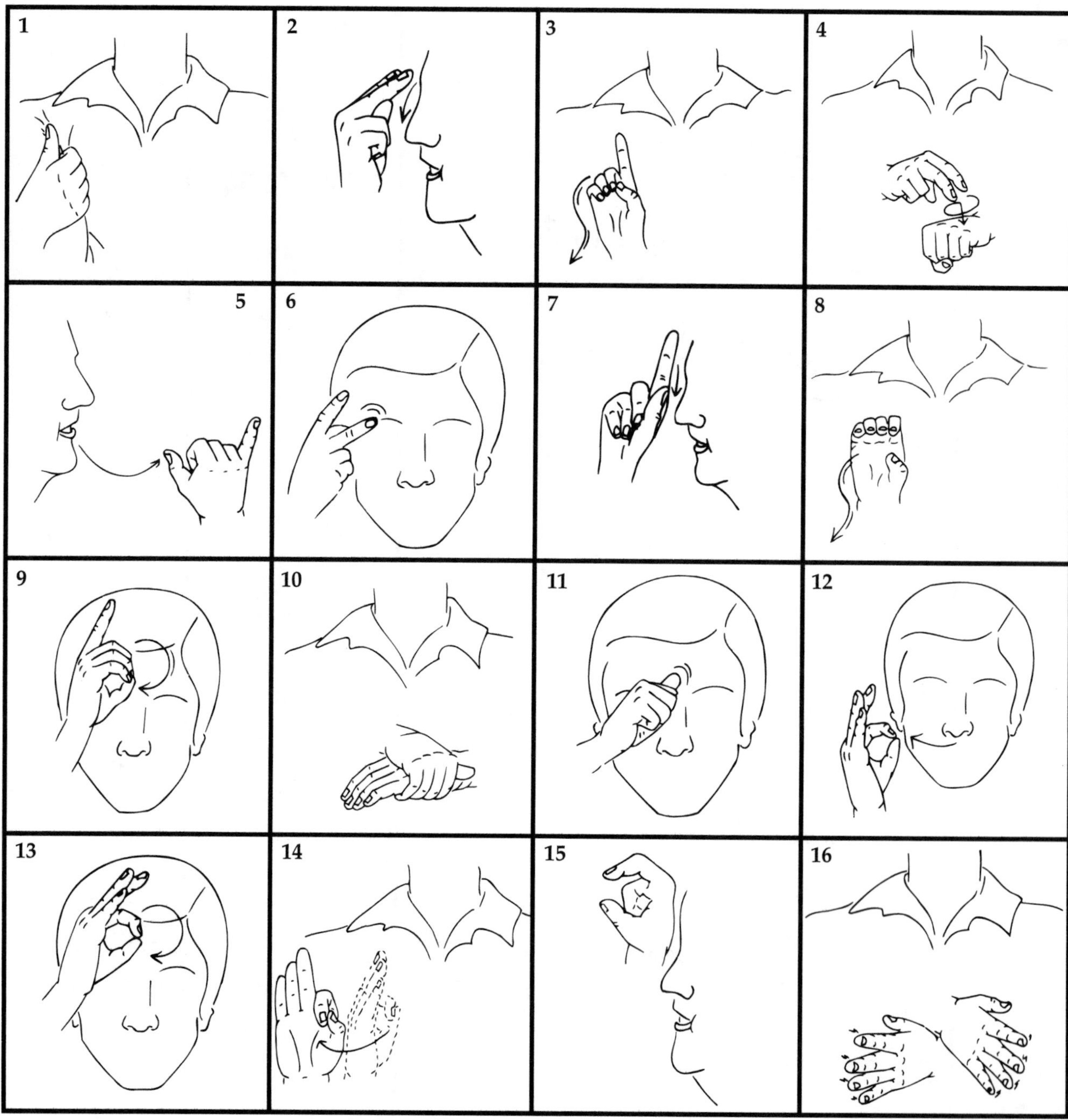

Countries, Cities, and States

On the previous page, write the meaning for each sign. Then find the words in the seek-a-word puzzle. The words may read forward, backward, up, down, or diagonally.

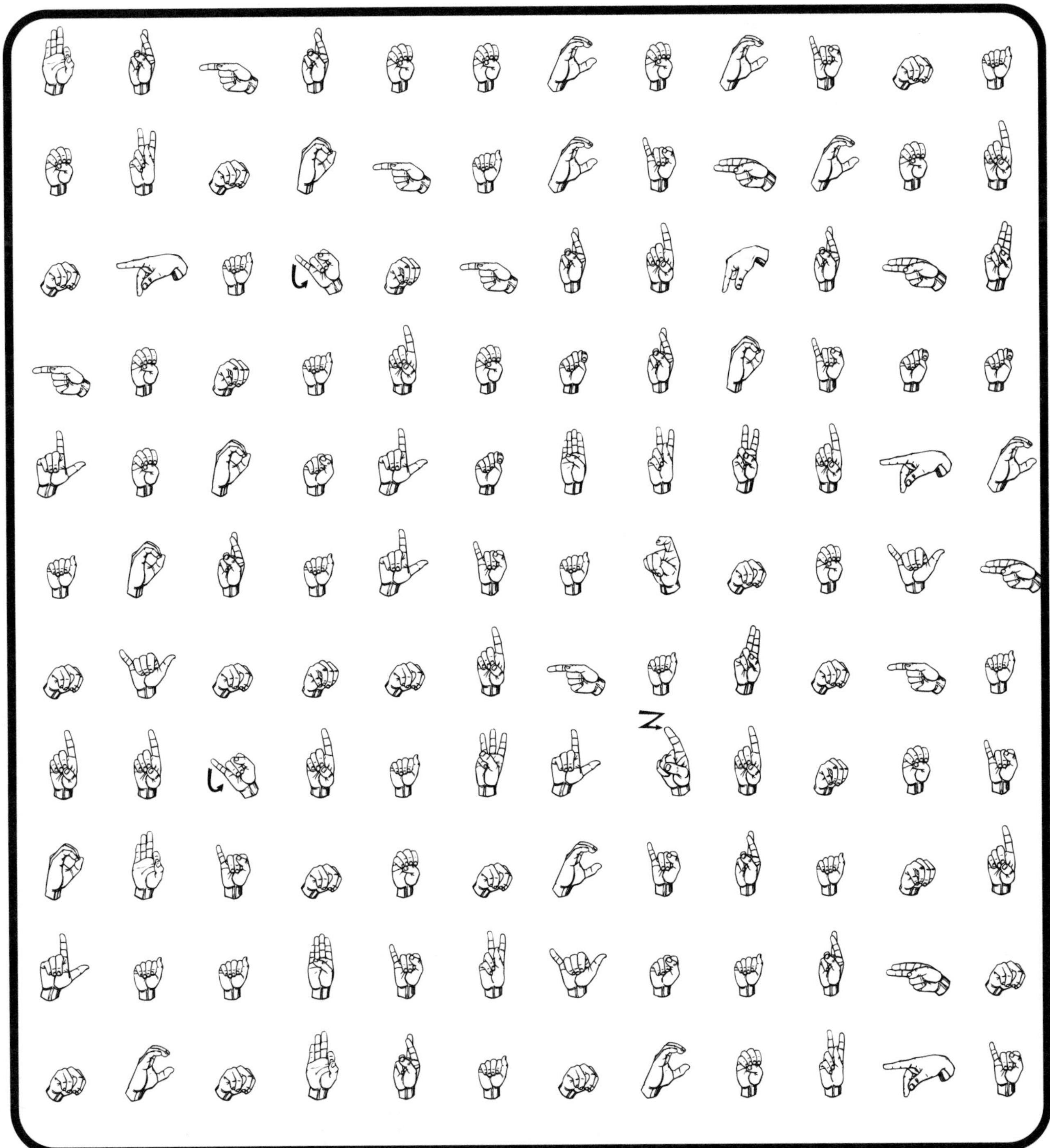

Chapter 23

Animals

Spell the word for the sign given; write the letter below each hand position.

1

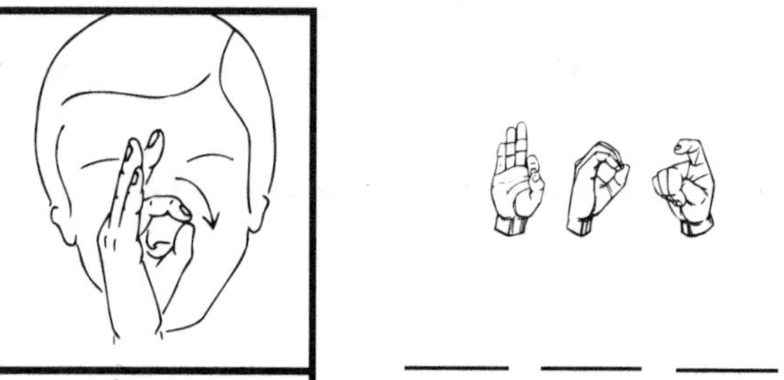

2

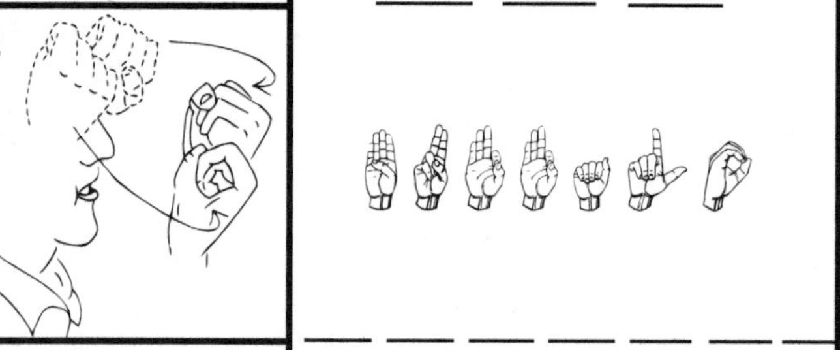

3

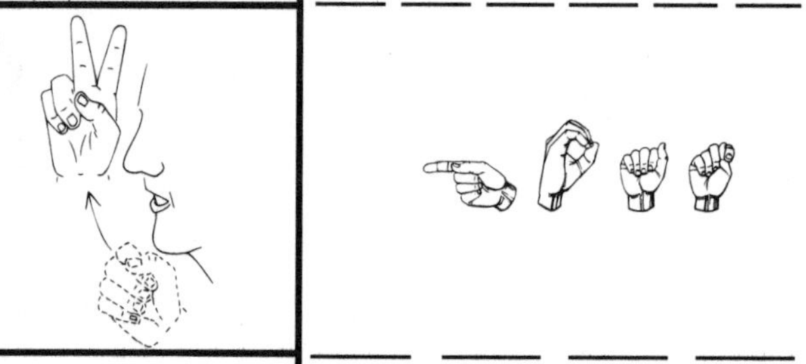

4

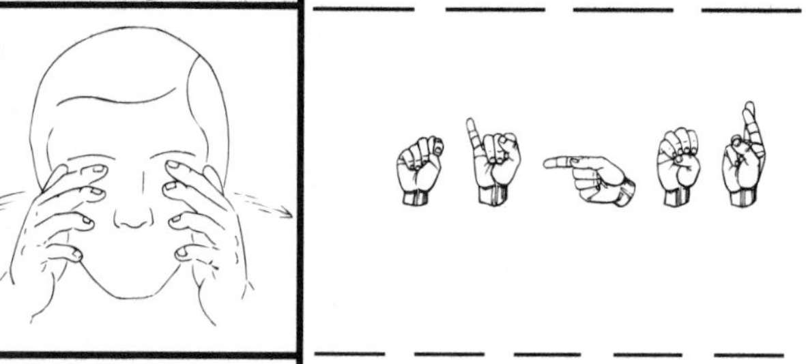

5

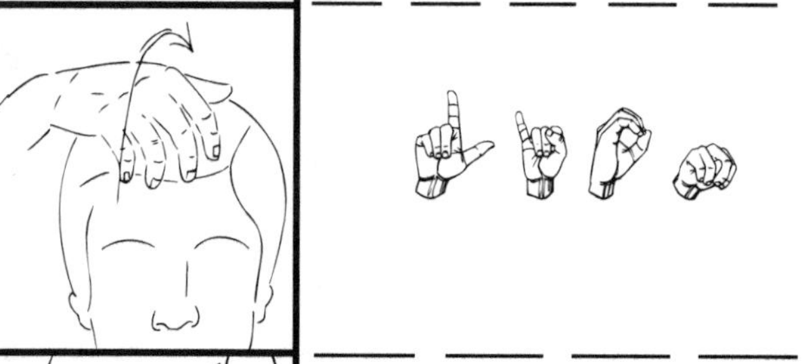

6

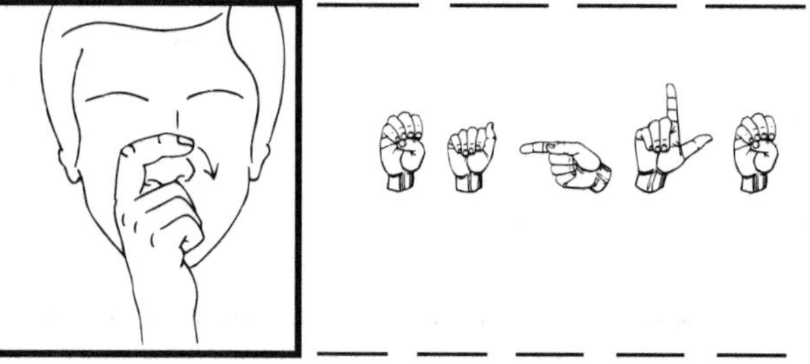

7

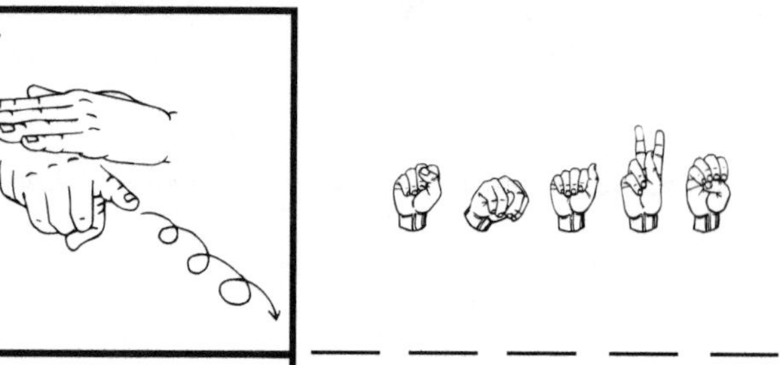

8

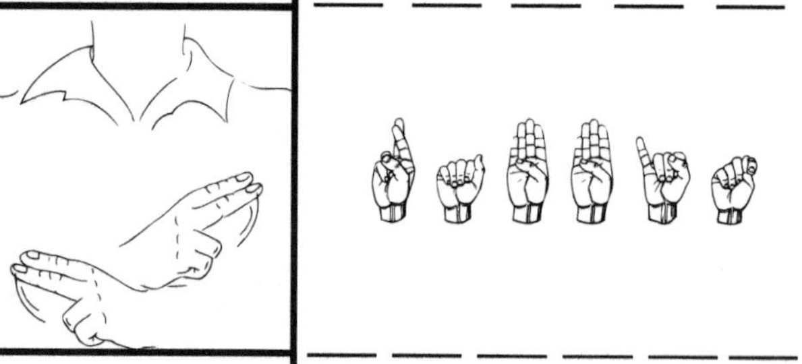

9

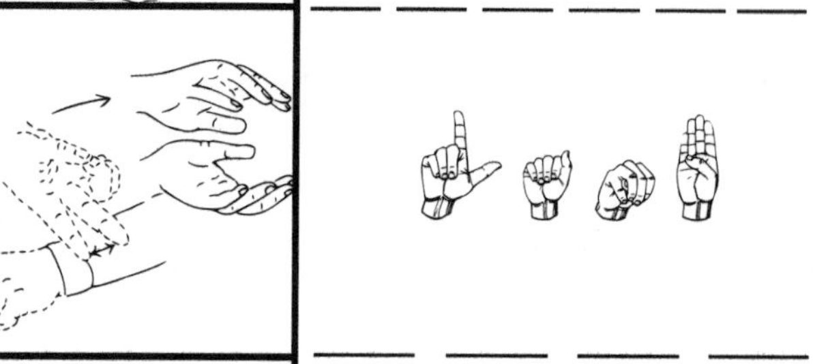

10

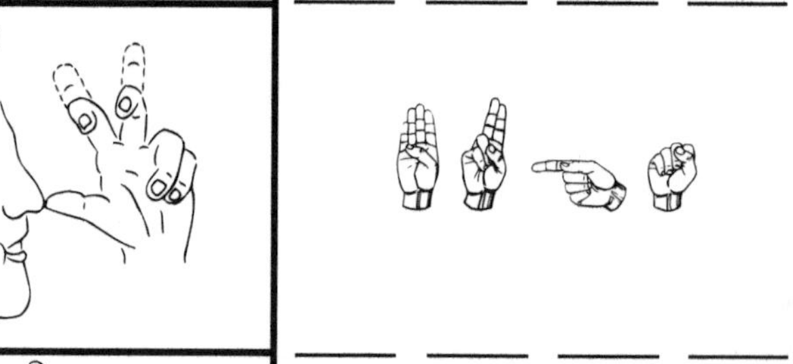

11

12

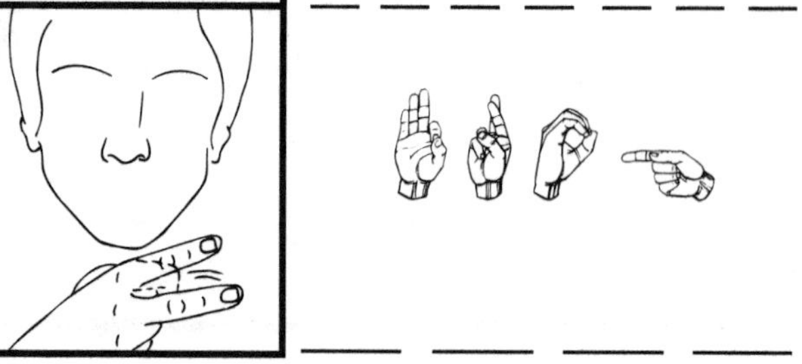

Match the sign with its origin and the fingerspelled word. Write the number (sign) and the letter (origin) in the corresponding fingerspelled box.

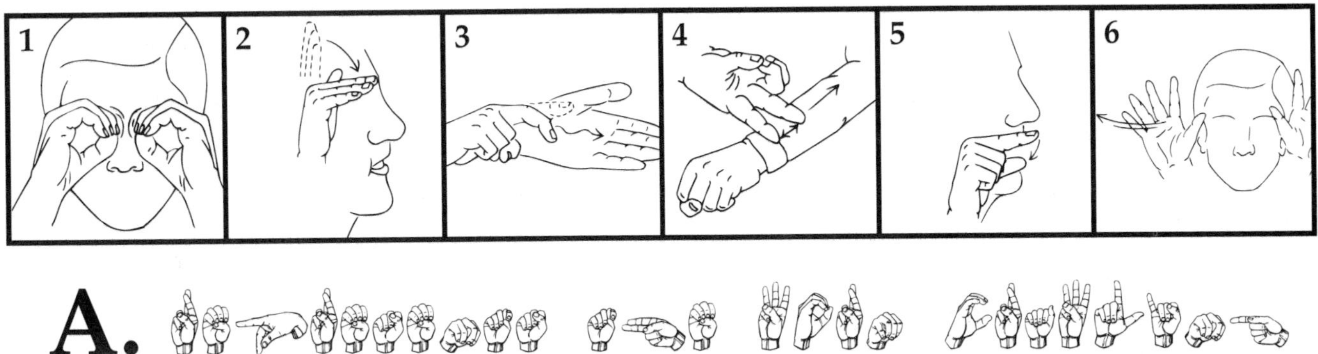

A. 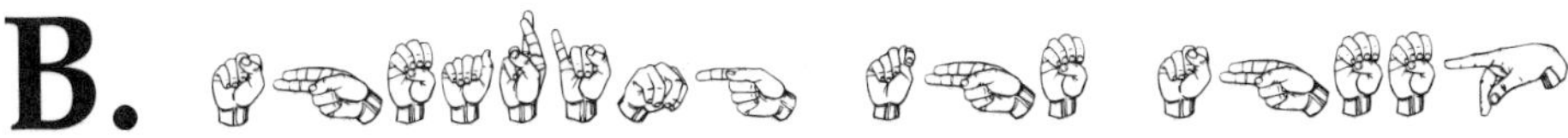

B. 

C.

D. 

E. 

F.

7	8	9
________ ________	________ ________	________ ________
10	11	12
________ ________	________ ________	________ ________

Chapter 24

Religion

Underline the word that matches the given sign.

1 A. Mission
B. Minister
C. Methodist

2 A. Thee
B. Thine
C. Heaven

3 A. Trinity
B. Tithe
C. Testament

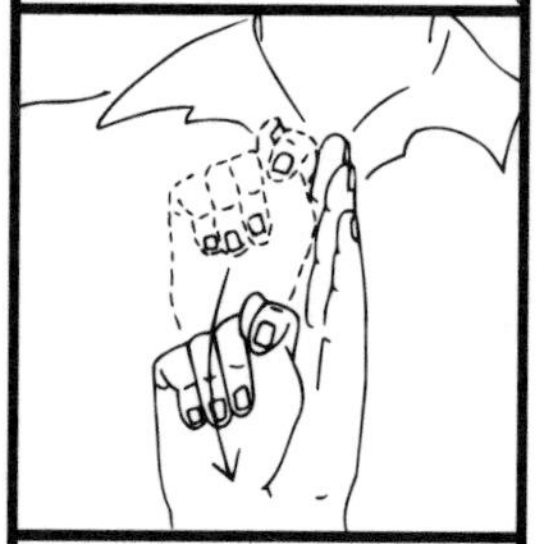

4 A. Ascension
B. Spirit
C. Soul

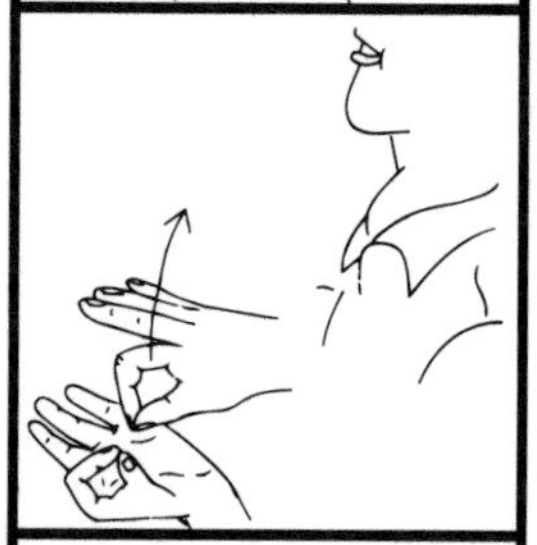

5 A. Save
B. Ascension
C. Sacrifice

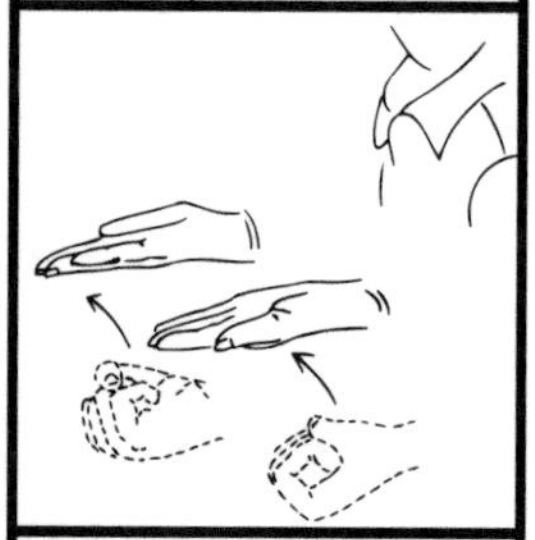

6 A. Hallelujah
B. Heaven
C. Pray

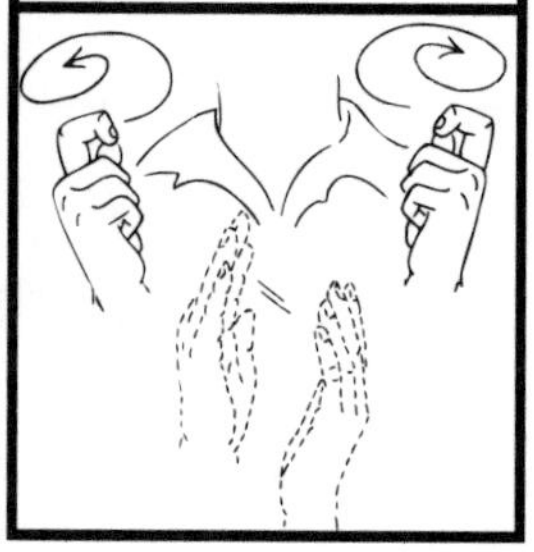

7 A. Pure
B. Passover
C. Protestant

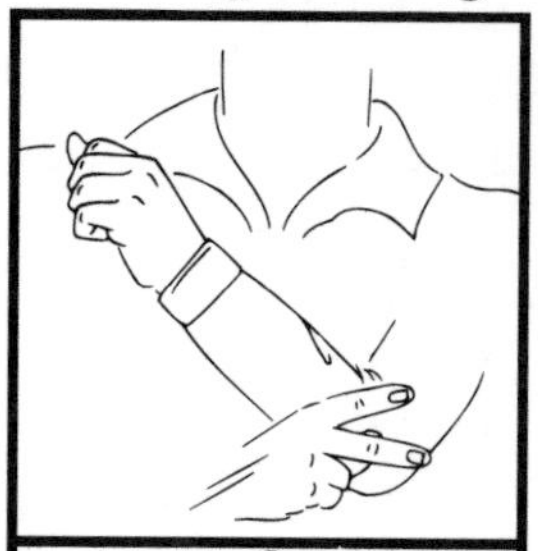

8 A. Christian
B. Church
C. Commandments

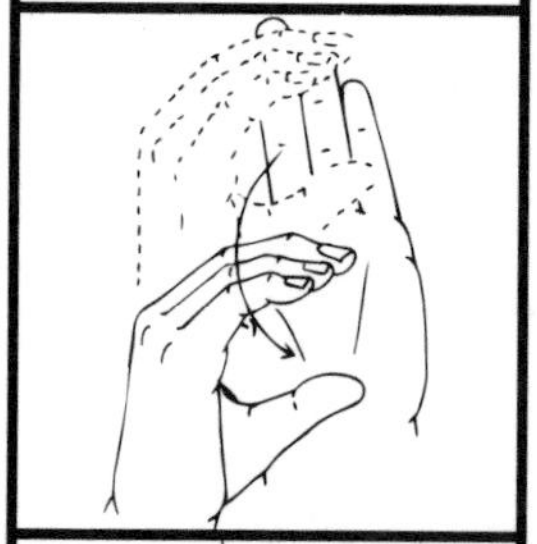

9 A. Revival
B. Repent
C. Redeem

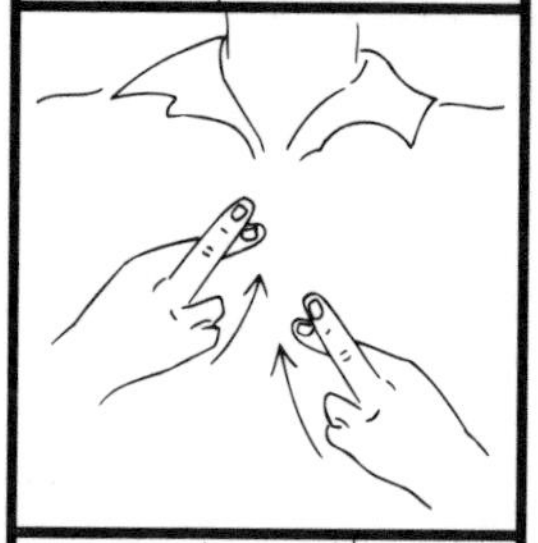

10 A. Will
B. Hanukkah
C. Miracle

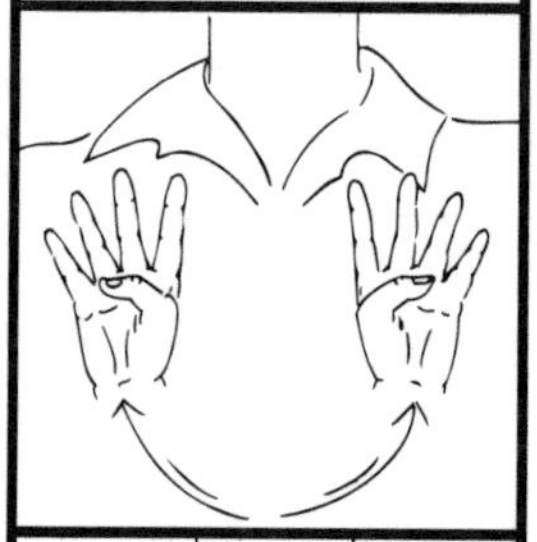

11 A. Grace
B. Gospel
C. Verse

12 A. Religion
B. Righteous
C. Repent

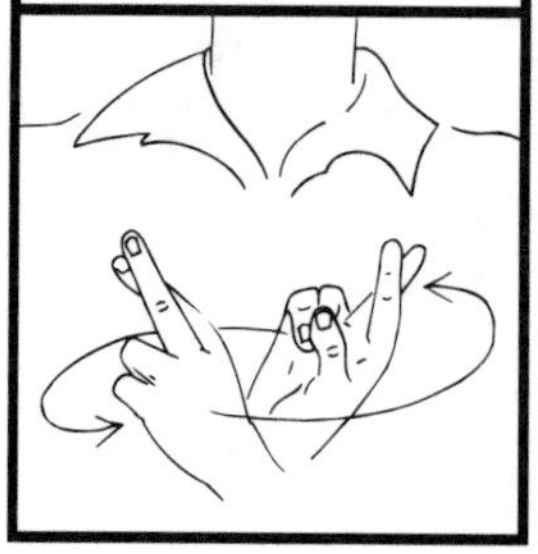

13
A. Save
B. Baptist
C. Baptize

14
A. Fast
B. Thee
C. Minister

15
A. Soul
B. Sacrifice
C. Anoint

16
A. Christian
B. Cross
C. Christmas

17
A. Save
B. Worship
C. Church

18

A. Cross
B. Repent
C. Crucify

19
A. Stand
B. Resurrection
C. Pray

20
A. Glory
B. Grace
C. Anoint

21
A. Heaven
B. Vision
C. Verse

22
A. Verse
B. Ghost
C. Grace

23
A. Amen
B. Bless
C. Be Seated

24
A. Holy
B. Hallelujah
C. Heaven

Chapter 24

ACROSS

Religion

On the previous page, write the meaning for each sign given. Then fill in the appropriate blanks in the crossword puzzle on this page.

Chapter 25

Numbers

Underline the word that matches the given sign.

1 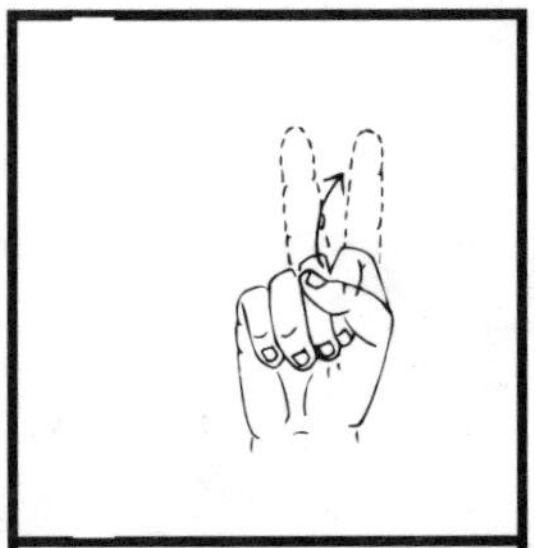
A. 2
B. 20
C. 12

2 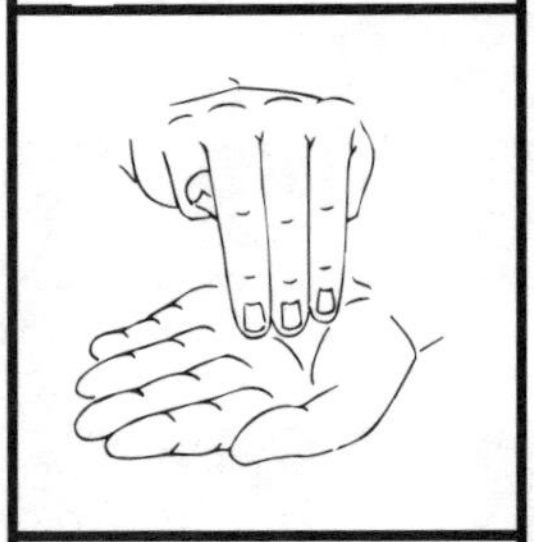
A. 3
B. Million
C. Thousand

3 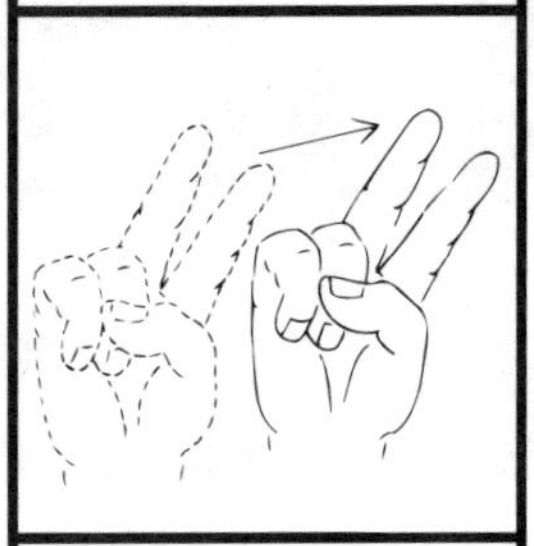
A. 4
B. 22
C. 12

4 
A. 33
B. 13
C. 6

5 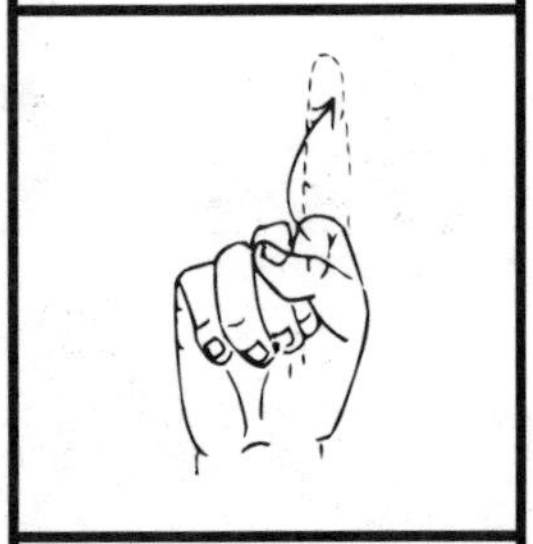
A. 11
B. 1
C. 100

6 
A. 13
B. 107
C. 17

7 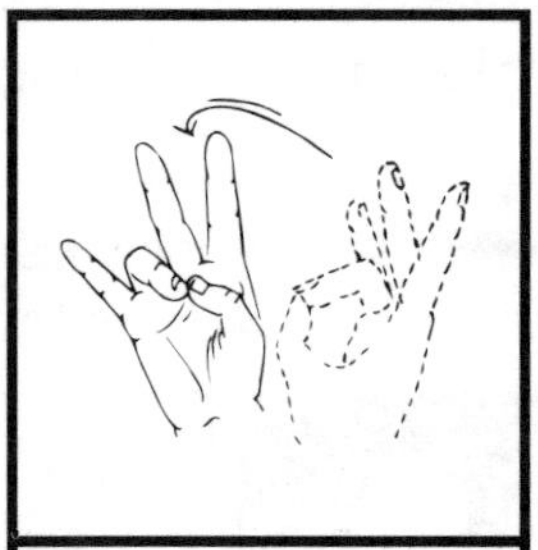
A. 77
B. 7th
C. 17

8 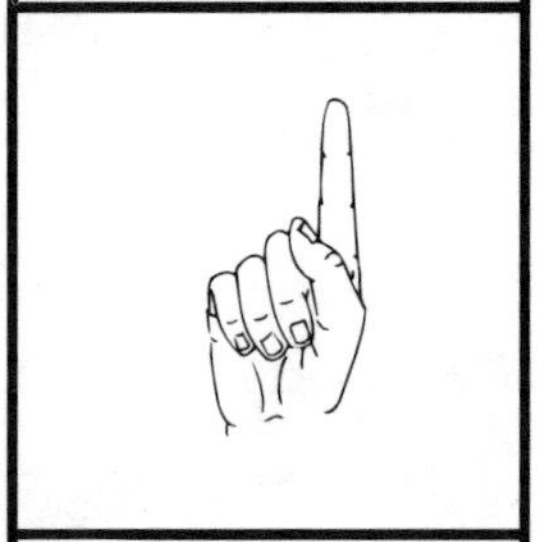
A. 1
B. 100
C. 1 cent

9 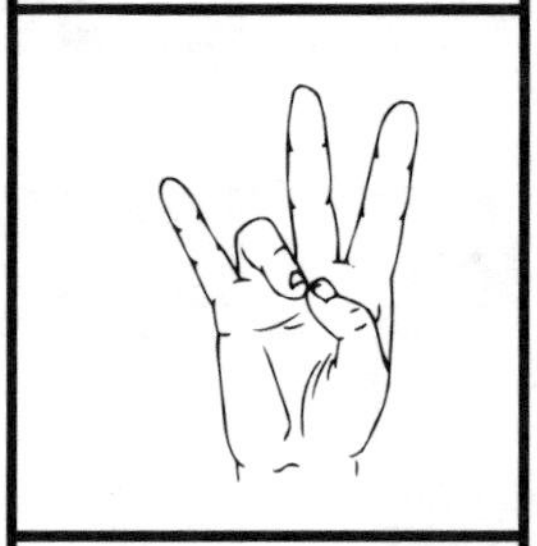
A. 7
B. 3
C. 12

10 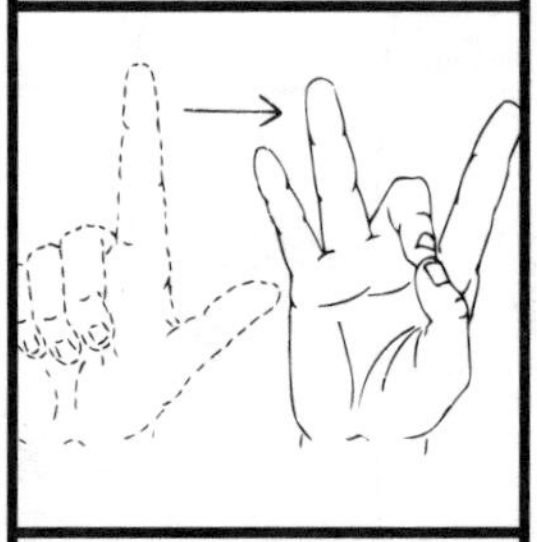
A. 28
B. 18
C. 23

11 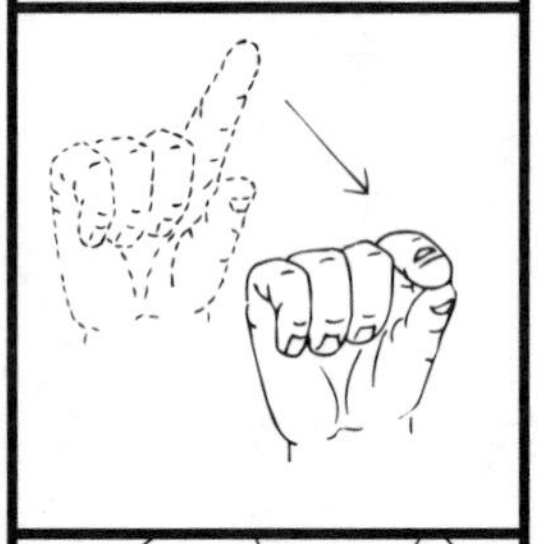
A. 10
B. 0
C. 20

12 
A. 18
B. $8.00
C. 80

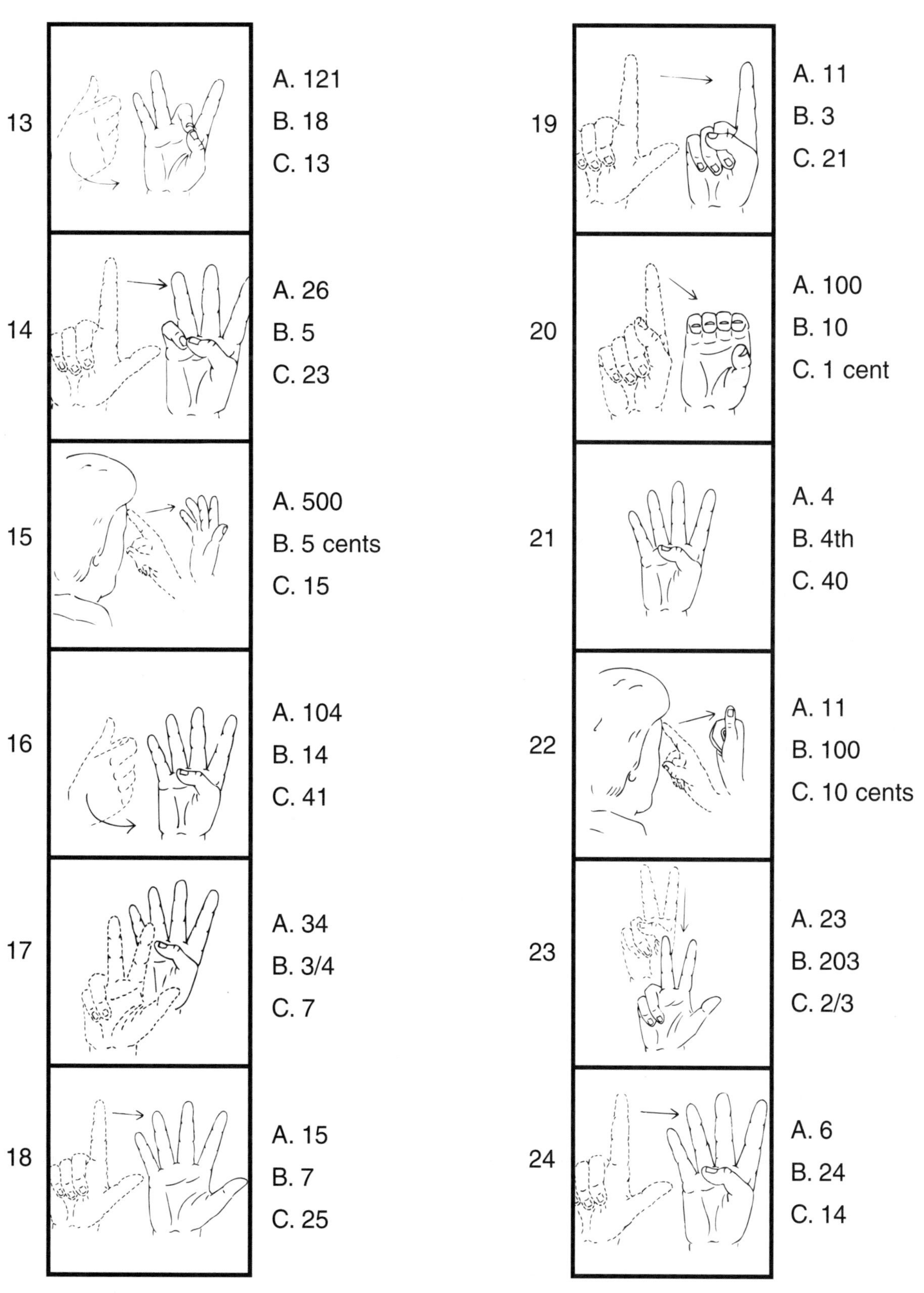
13
A. 121
B. 18
C. 13
14
A. 26
B. 5
C. 23
15
A. 500
B. 5 cents
C. 15
16
A. 104
B. 14
C. 41
17
A. 34
B. 3/4
C. 7
18
A. 15
B. 7
C. 25
19
A. 11
B. 3
C. 21
20
A. 100
B. 10
C. 1 cent
21
A. 4
B. 4th
C. 40
22
A. 11
B. 100
C. 10 cents
23
A. 23
B. 203
C. 2/3
24
A. 6
B. 24
C. 14

Chapter 25

Numbers

On the previous page, write the meaning for each sign. Then find the words in the seek-a-word puzzle. The words may read forward, backward, up, down, or diagonally.

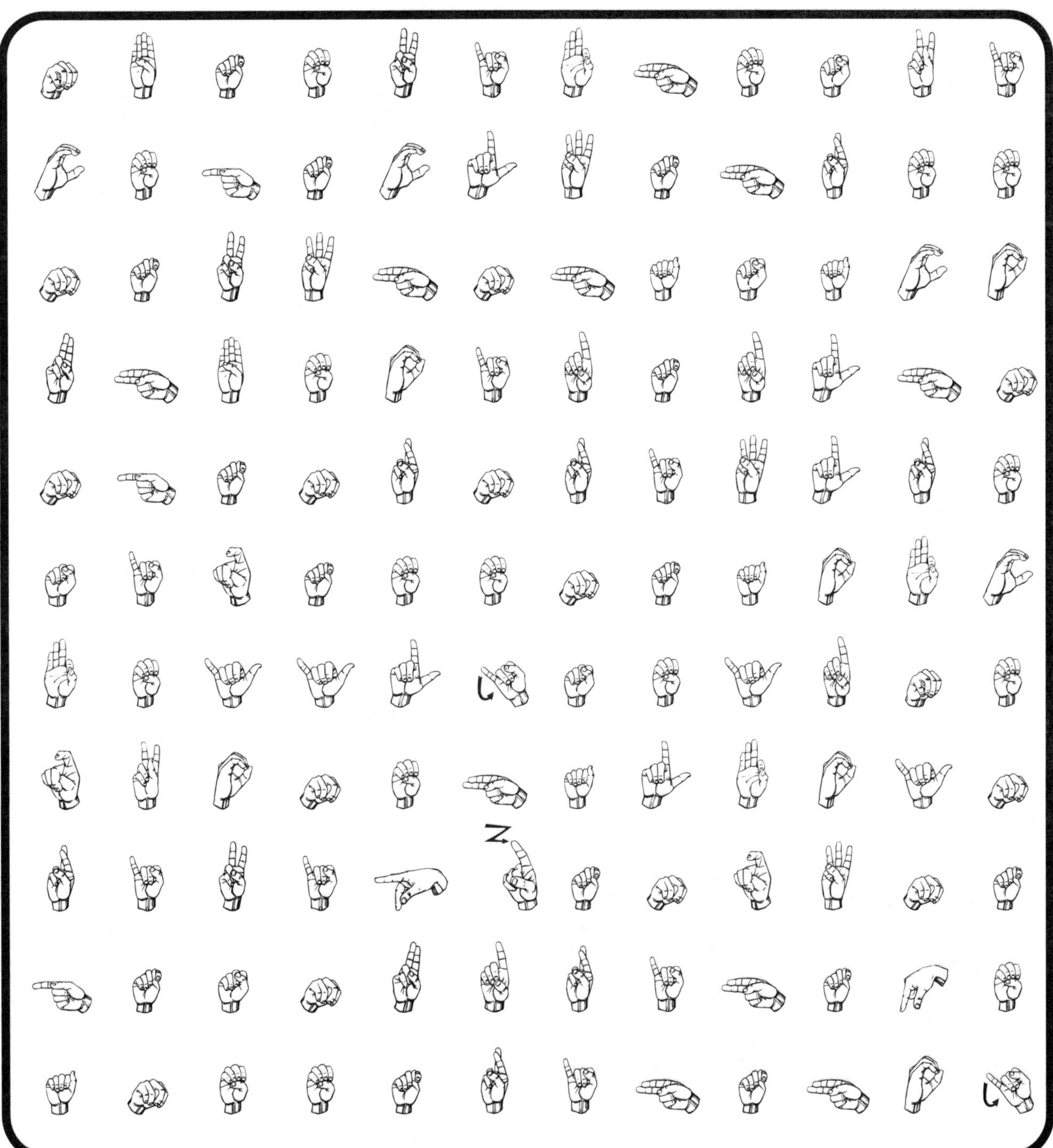

Answers

Chapter 1

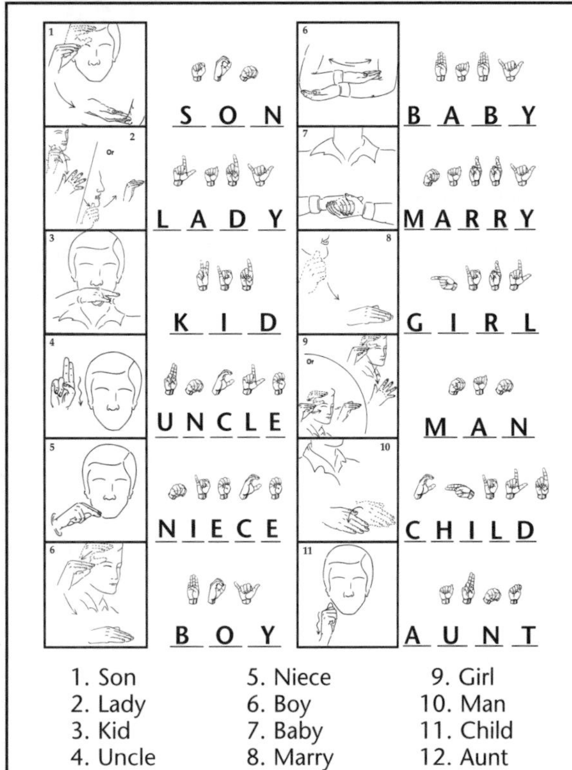

1. Son
2. Lady
3. Kid
4. Uncle
5. Niece
6. Boy
7. Baby
8. Marry
9. Girl
10. Man
11. Child
12. Aunt

page 11

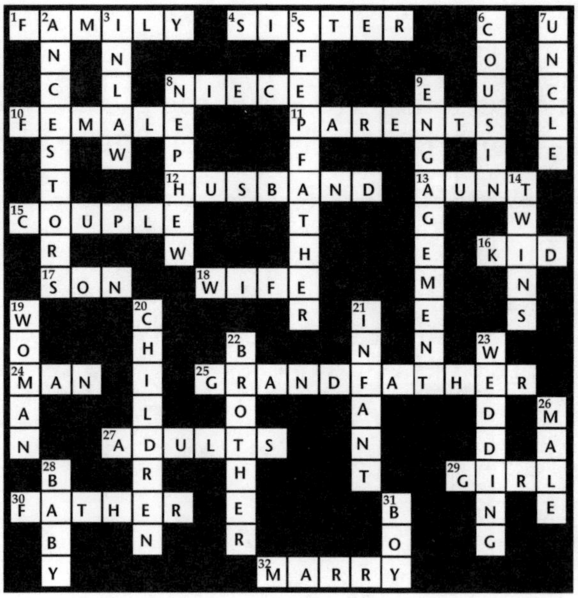

page 13

Chapter 2

page 15

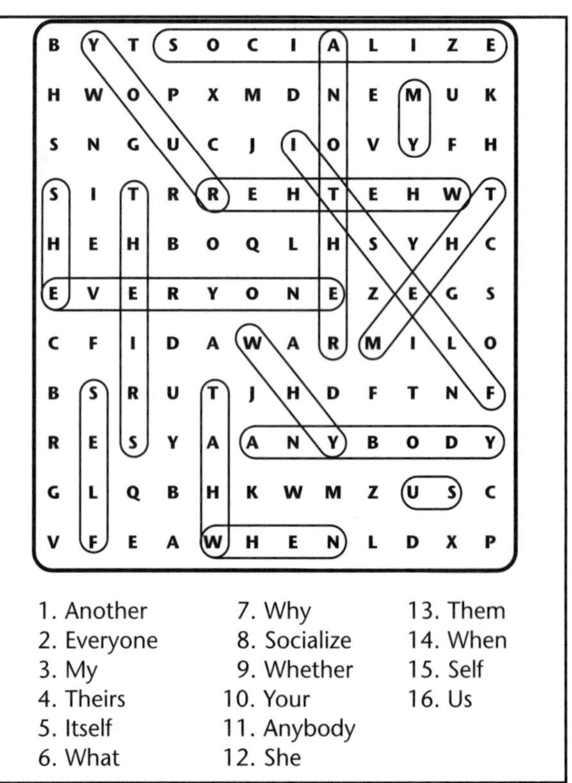

1. Another
2. Everyone
3. My
4. Theirs
5. Itself
6. What
7. Why
8. Socialize
9. Whether
10. Your
11. Anybody
12. She
13. Them
14. When
15. Self
16. Us

page 17

CHAPTER 3

page 19

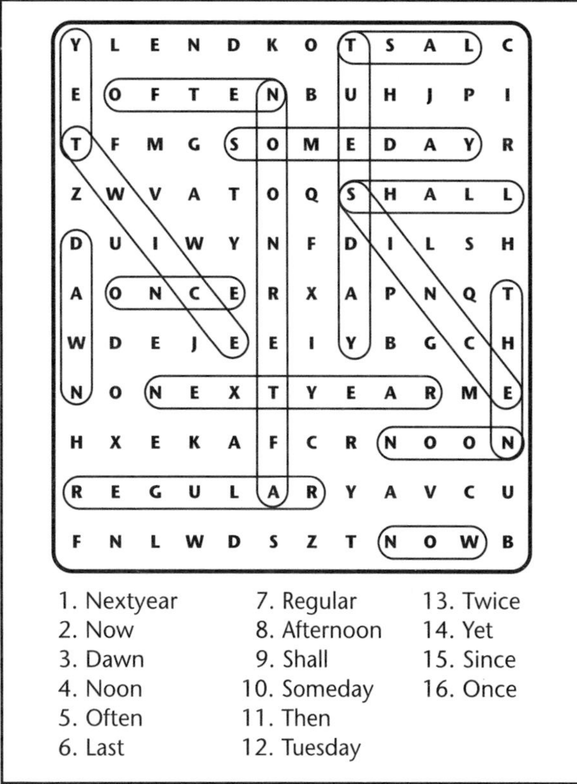

page 21

CHAPTER 4

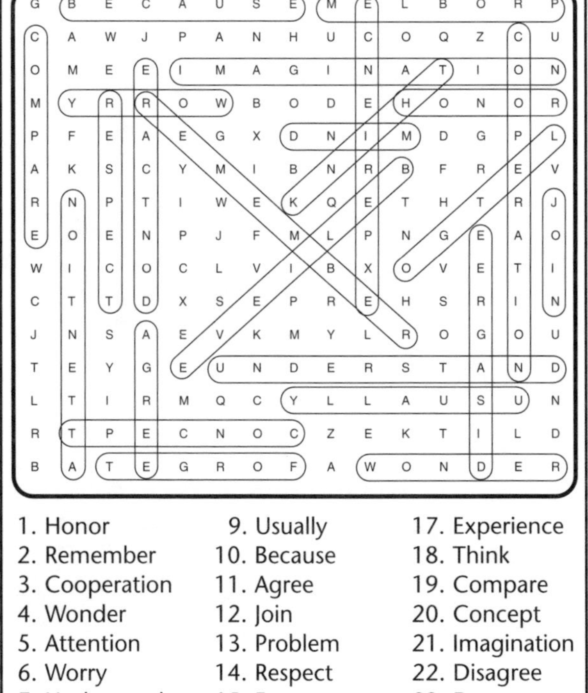

page 23

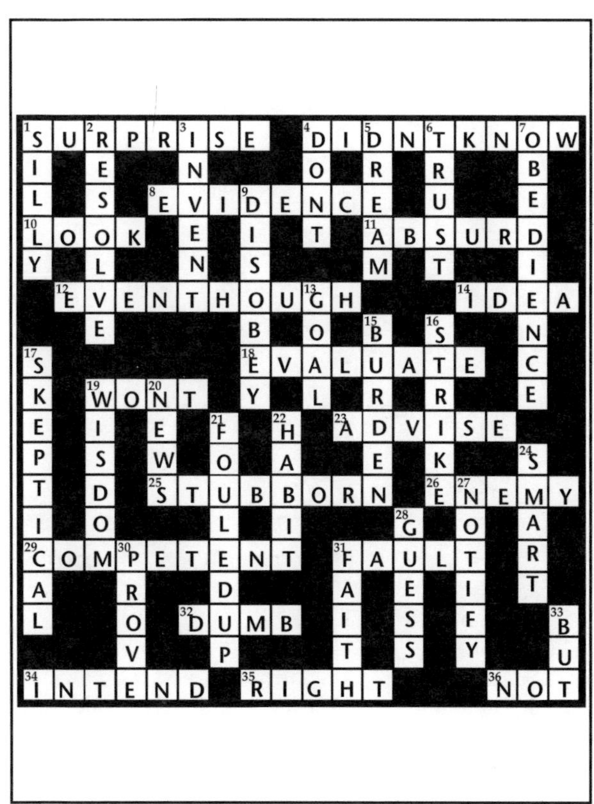

page 25

CHAPTER 5

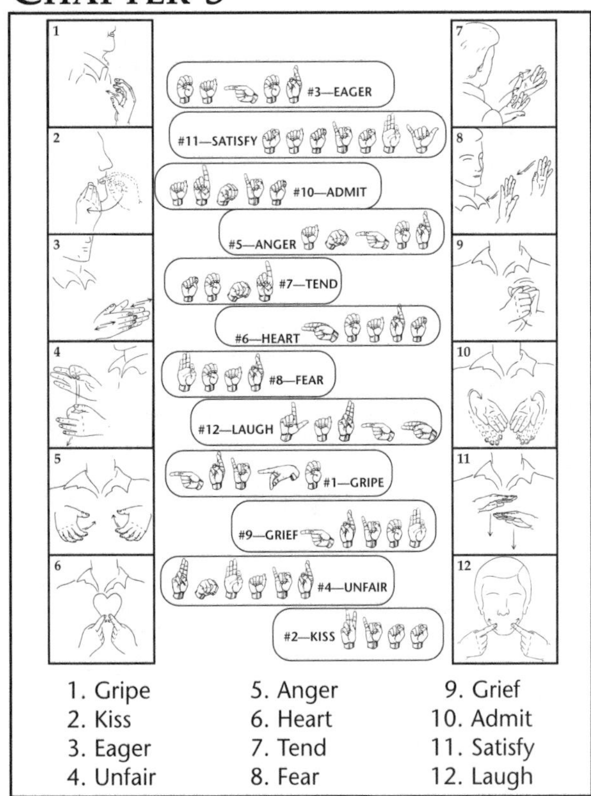

1. Gripe
2. Kiss
3. Eager
4. Unfair
5. Anger
6. Heart
7. Tend
8. Fear
9. Grief
10. Admit
11. Satisfy
12. Laugh

page 26

A. **inner turmoil**
B. **the fluttering eyelashes**
C. **face becoming red**
D. **smiling from ear to ear**
E. **a handshake of peace**
F. **self pushed forward**

7 peace 5 E	8 brag 4 F	9 blush 1 C
10 smile 2 D	11 flirt 6 B	12 agony 3 A

page 27

CHAPTER 6

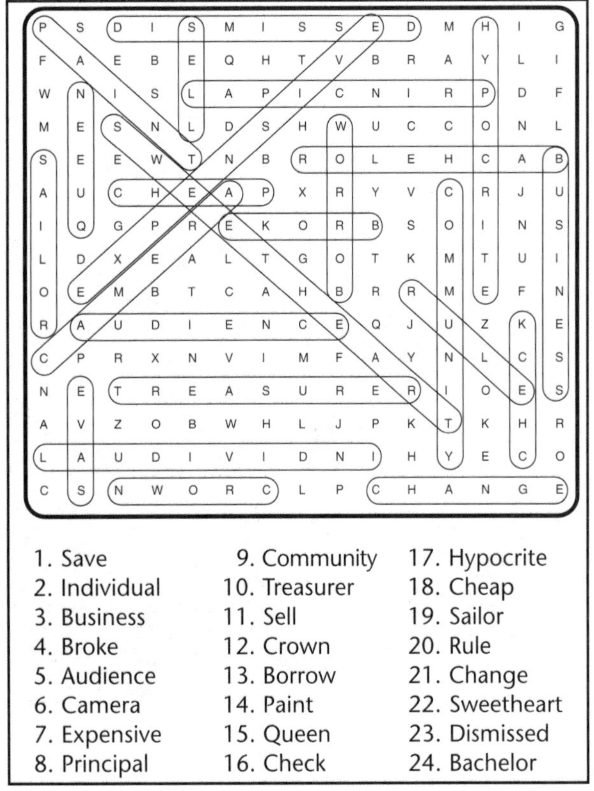

1. Save
2. Individual
3. Business
4. Broke
5. Audience
6. Camera
7. Expensive
8. Principal
9. Community
10. Treasurer
11. Sell
12. Crown
13. Borrow
14. Paint
15. Queen
16. Check
17. Hypocrite
18. Cheap
19. Sailor
20. Rule
21. Change
22. Sweetheart
23. Dismissed
24. Bachelor

page 29

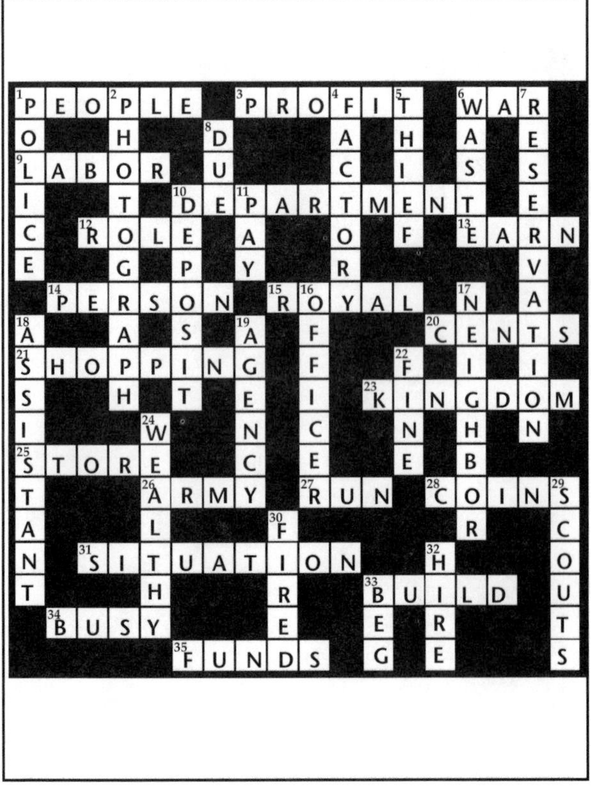

page 31

CHAPTER 7

page 33

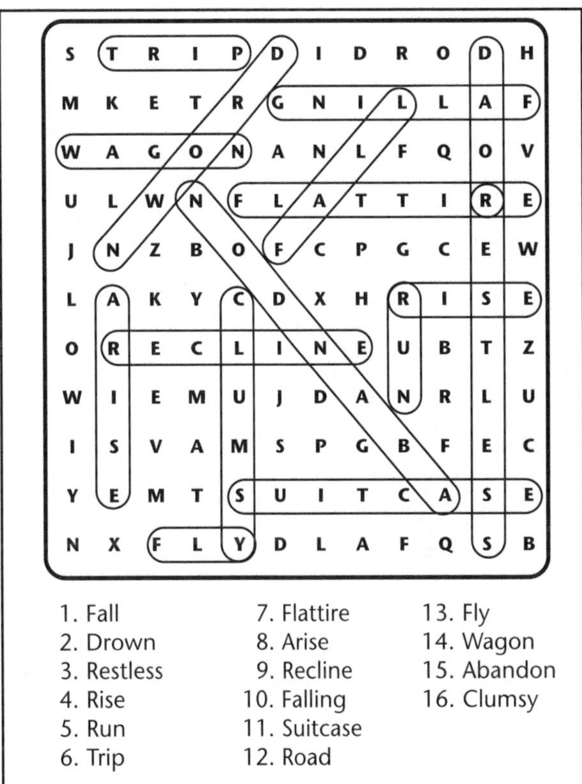

page 35

CHAPTER 8

1. B—Always
2. A—Up
3. C—Behind
4. B—Join
5. B—Lights On
6. C—Dark
7. B—Quick
8. A—Ask
9. B—Light
10. C—Negative
11. A—Long
12. B—Right

page 36

13. B—Quit
14. C—Lights Out
15. A—Stop
16. C—Possible
17. B—Right
18. C—Condense
19. B—Open-minded
20. C—Difficult
21. B—Went
22. A—In
23. C—Narrow-minded
24. A—Short

page 37

CHAPTER 8 CONTINUED

page 39

CHAPTER 9

page 41

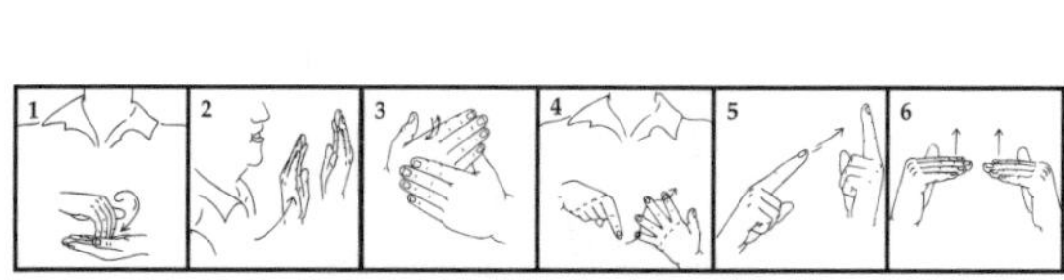

A. **being elevated**

B. **heading toward an object**

C. **in the center of the hand**

D. **hands facing each other**

E. **in and out among the fingers**

F. **between the thumb and fingers**

7 between	8 high	9 before
3 F	6 A	2 D
10 toward	11 center	12 among
5 B	1 C	4 E

page 42

CHAPTER 10

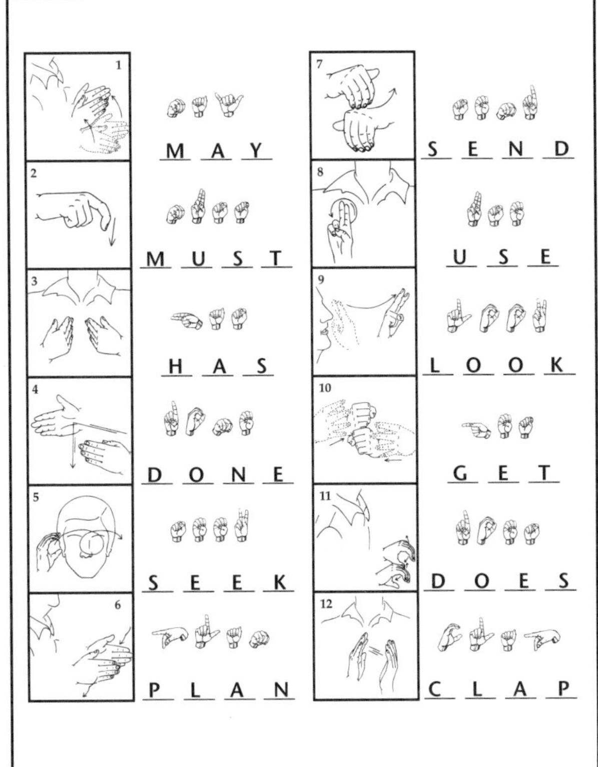

page 43

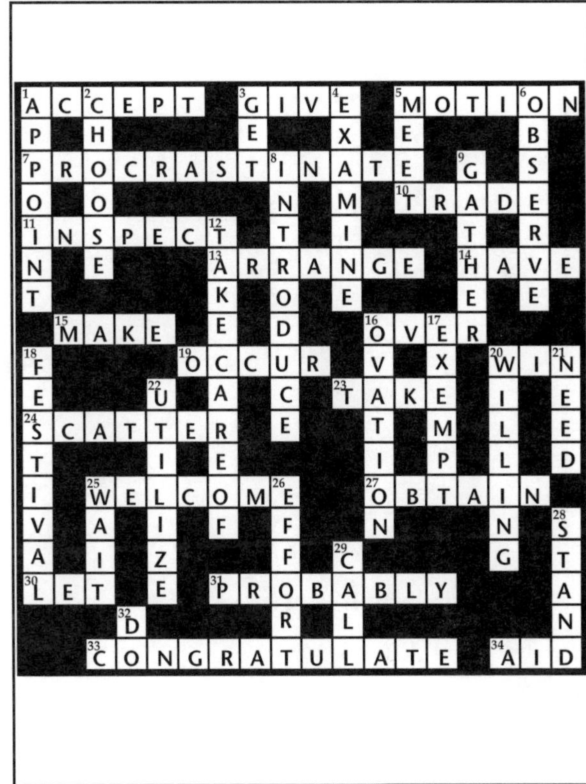

page 45

CHAPTER 11

page 47

W	R	R	E	T	U	P	J	T	F	J	T
D	E	S	T	R	O	Y	R	R	A	C	L
Y	J	U	G	I	O	M	C	H	I	T	Z
N	E	E	D	X	C	Y	G	Q	L	E	S
H	C	S	O	B	L	E	N	D	W	M	A
N	T	F	U	H	A	V	I	C	K	P	X
F	O	R	C	E	E	P	T	D	F	T	B
A	F	H	M	G	R	K	A	G	B	V	Y
H	R	S	H	E	L	T	E	R	I	D	N
C	A	U	S	E	Z	A	B	L	A	M	E
E	B	P	I	L	G	L	Q	Y	N	E	D

1. Blame
2. Beating
3. Destroy
4. Tempt
5. Blend
6. Force
7. Deny
8. Urge
9. Shelter
10. Push
11. Hit
12. Reject
13. Deny
14. Cause
15. Carry
16. Fail

page 49

Chapter 12

1. A—Color
2. C—Weak
3. A—Confusion
4. B—Fine
5. A—Vibration
6. C—Sharp
7. C—Strong
8. A—Blue
9. B—Curious
10. A—Wonderful
11. B—Specific
12. C—Dry

page 50

13. B—Fun
14. A—Kind
15. A—Yellow
16. B—Worthless
17. B—Danger
18. C—Shining
19. C—Clean
20. A—Alike
21. B—Variety
22. A—Gray
23. B—Opposite
24. B—Pet

page 51

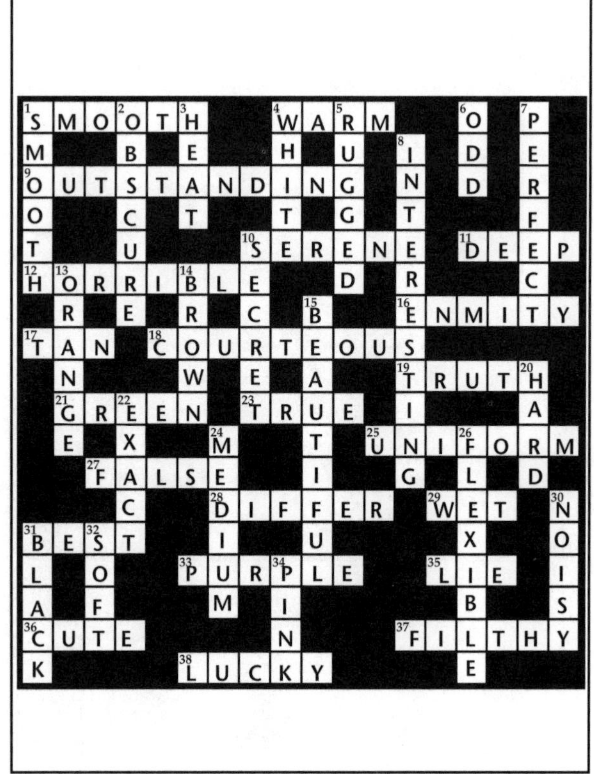

page 53

CHAPTER 13

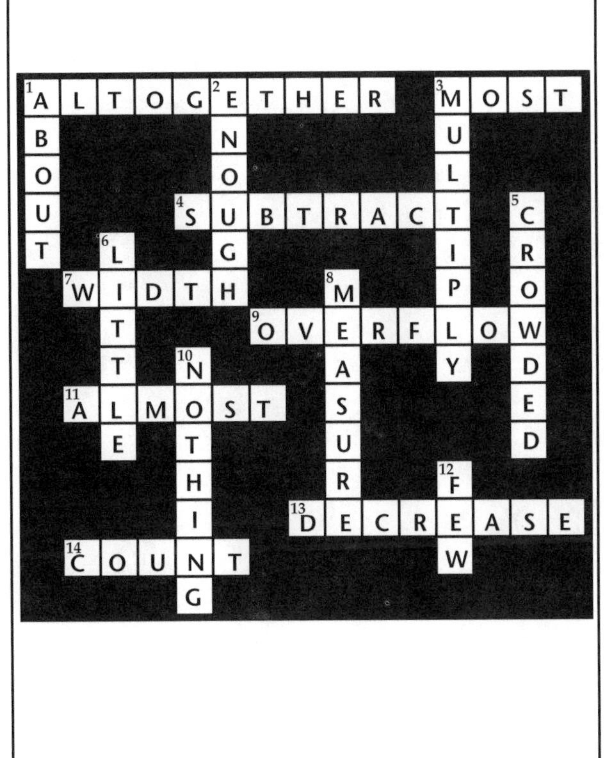

page 55

A. indicating a part of the whole

B. one hand lower than the other

C. as if splitting something

D. filled up to the chin

E. indicating a scale balancing

F. filled to the brim

7 divide	8 under	9 full
4 C	6 B	3 D
10 part	11 weigh	12 full
2 A	1 E	5 F

page 56

CHAPTER 14

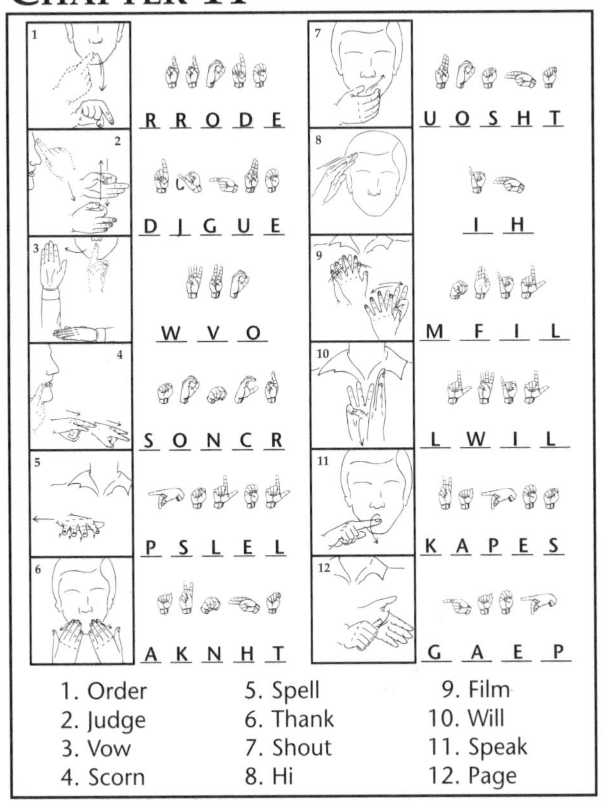

1. Order
2. Judge
3. Vow
4. Scorn
5. Spell
6. Thank
7. Shout
8. Hi
9. Film
10. Will
11. Speak
12. Page

page 57

page 59

Chapter 15

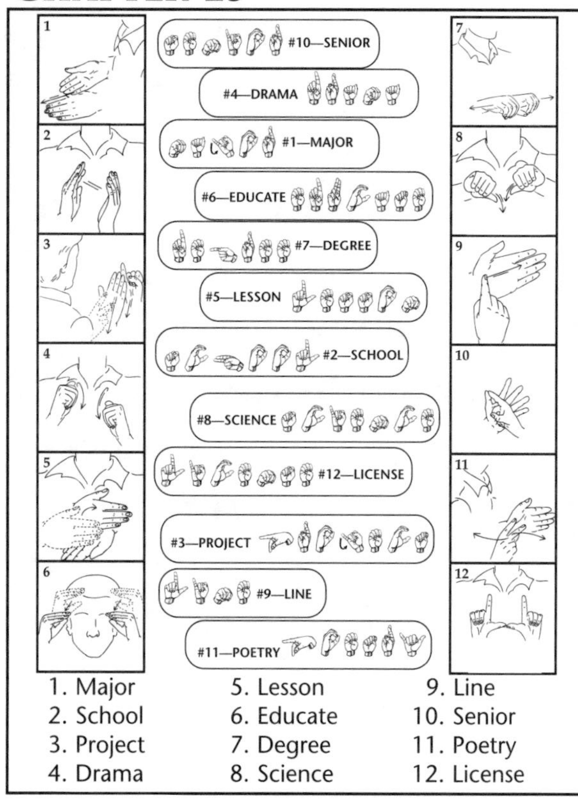

page 60

A. **wheels of progress**
B. **as if drawing a picture**
C. **poring over a book**
D. **all questions coming at you**
E. **directing the music**
F. **a school that is higher**

7 music	8 college	9 process
6 E	1 F	5 A
10 quiz	11 study	12 design
2 D	4 C	3 B

page 61

Chapter 16

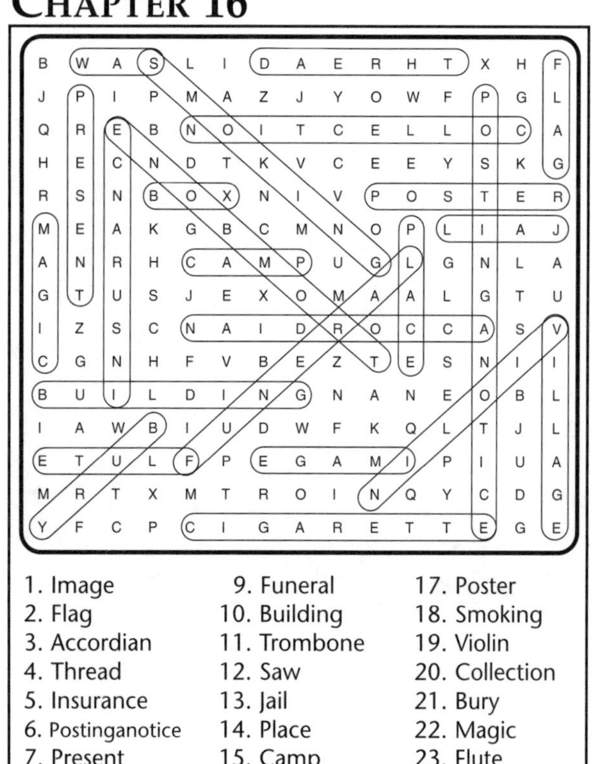

page 63

page 65

CHAPTER 17

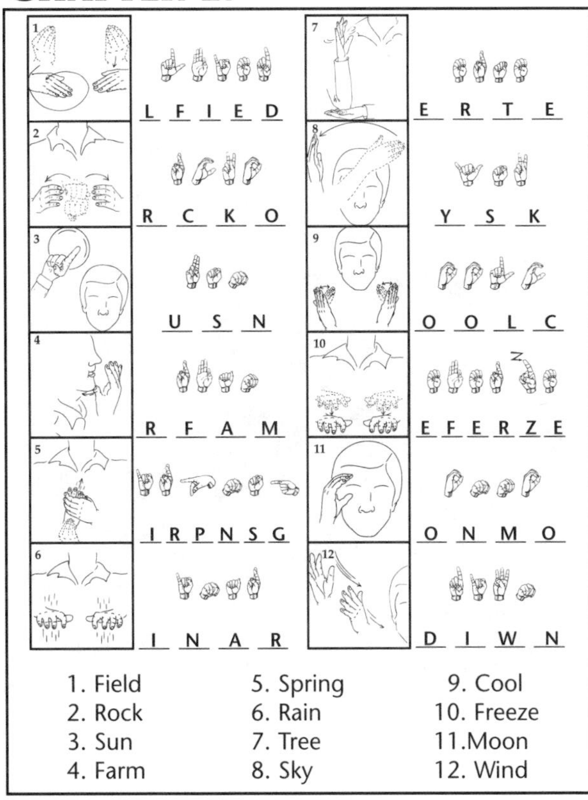

page 66

A. **the water level is rising**

B. **indicating billows of clouds**

C. **planting seeds in a row**

D. **the world going around**

E. **water and waves**

F. **water that flows**

7 plant	8 world	9 cloud
2 C	5 D	3 B
10 flow	11 ocean	12 flood
1 F	6 E	4 A

page 67

CHAPTER 18

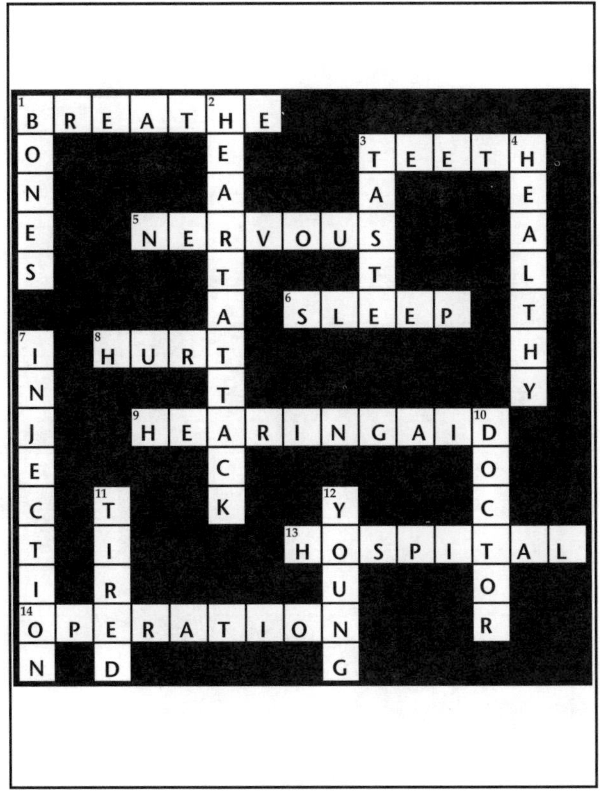

page 69

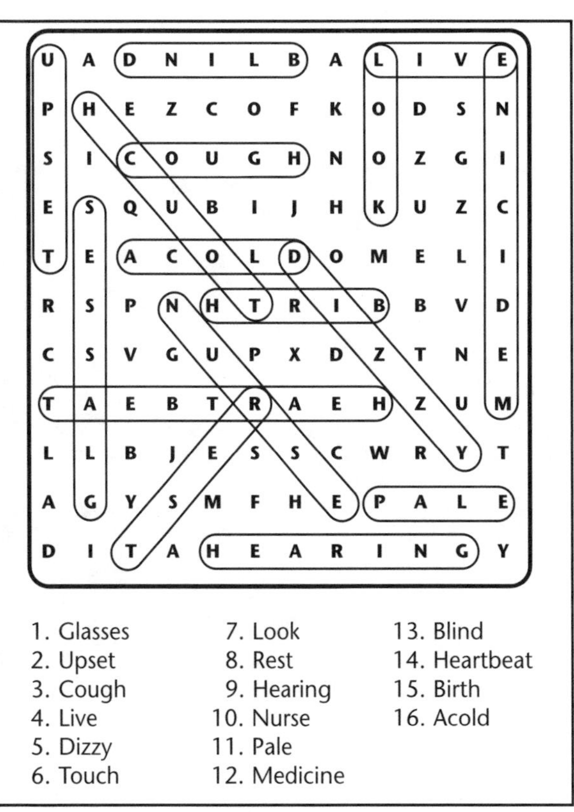

page 71

Chapter 19

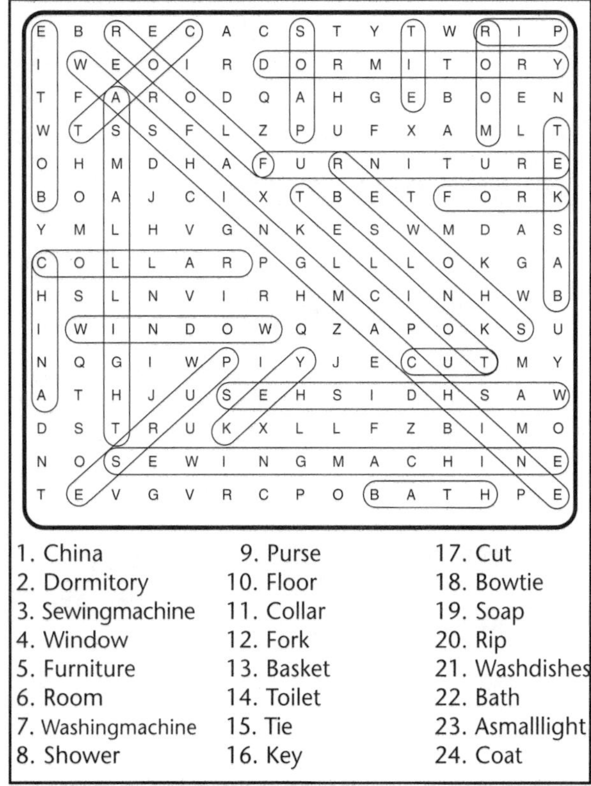

1. China
2. Dormitory
3. Sewingmachine
4. Window
5. Furniture
6. Room
7. Washingmachine
8. Shower
9. Purse
10. Floor
11. Collar
12. Fork
13. Basket
14. Toilet
15. Tie
16. Key
17. Cut
18. Bowtie
19. Soap
20. Rip
21. Washdishes
22. Bath
23. Asmalllight
24. Coat

page 73

1 DISHES, 3 HANDBAG, 6 BED, 8 APARTMENT, 10 TROUSERS, 11 BLOUSE, 14 GOWN, 15 DRYER, 17 CUP, 19 GATE, 20 CLOTHES, 21 PLATE, 22 IRONING, 24 SPOON, 25 SEW, 27 SHOES, 30 TOOTHBRUSH, 31 NECKTIE, 32 HOSE, 33 REFRIGERATOR

page 75

Chapter 20

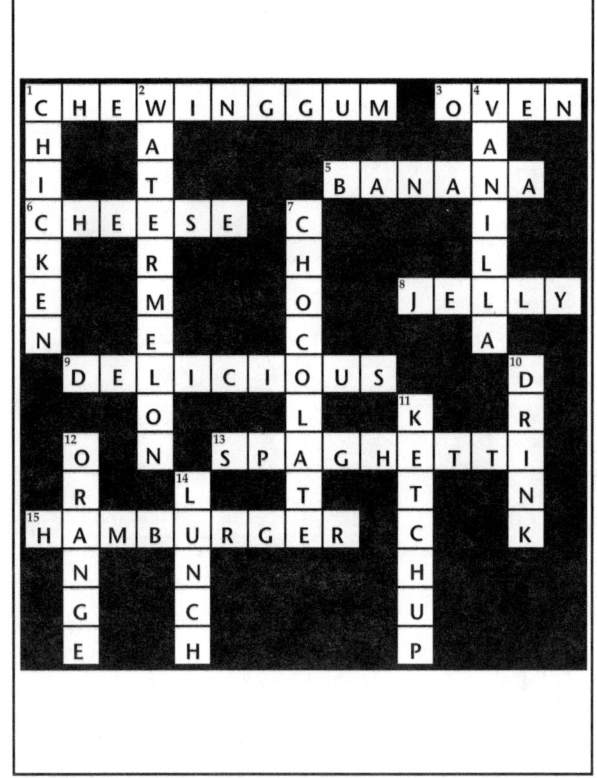

page 77

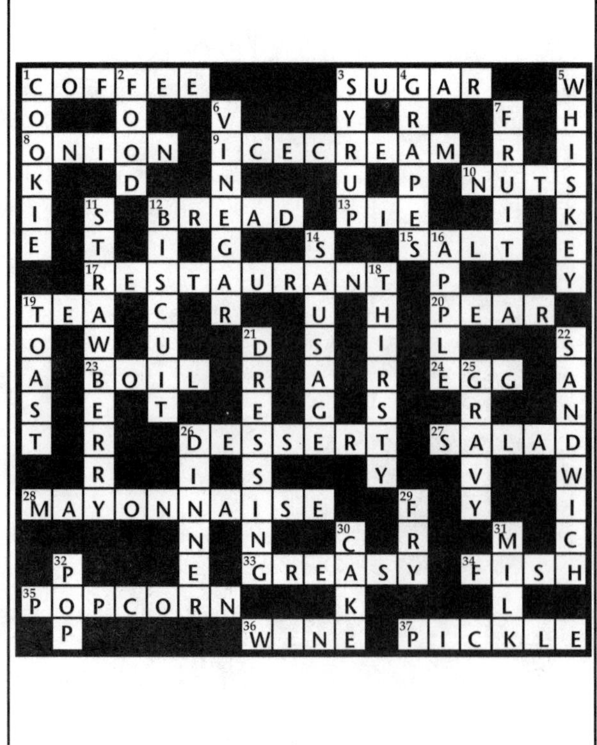

page 79

CHAPTER 21

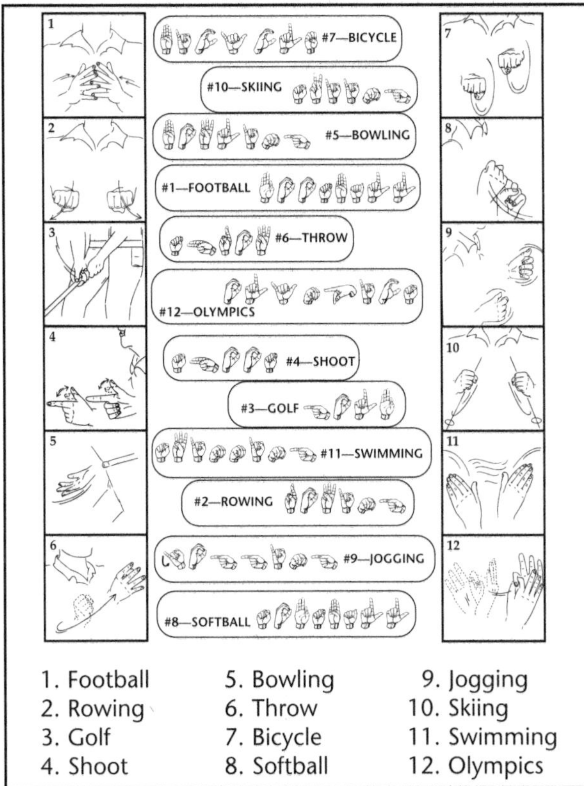

1. Football
2. Rowing
3. Golf
4. Shoot
5. Bowling
6. Throw
7. Bicycle
8. Softball
9. Jogging
10. Skiing
11. Swimming
12. Olympics

page 80

A. the sign for play is initialed

B. two sides facing each other in competition

C. activity indicated by the hands

D. the motions of boxing

E. first one gets ahead, then the other

F. pulling up on the line

7 game	8 race	9 fishing
3 B	1 E	5 F
10 party	11 boxing	12 play
2 A	6 D	4 C

page 81

CHAPTER 22

1. B—Europe
2. B—Country
3. A—Sweden
4. C—Washington
5. B—Israel
6. B—Boston
7. A—Spain
8. B—International
9. B—Switzerland
10. C—Australia
11. A—Italy
12. A—Philippine Islands

page 82

13. A—Russia
14. B—China
15. C—California
16. A—Scotland
17. C—Norway
18. B—New York
19. A—Mexico
20. C—Africa
21. C—Holland
22. B—Hawaii
23. A—America
24. C—Minneapolis

page 83

Chapter 22 Continued

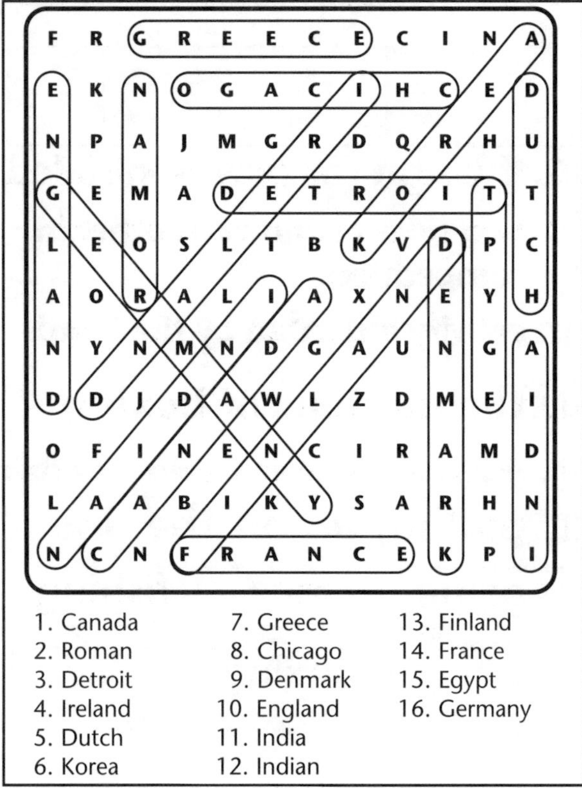

1. Canada	7. Greece	13. Finland
2. Roman	8. Chicago	14. France
3. Detroit	9. Denmark	15. Egypt
4. Ireland	10. England	16. Germany
5. Dutch	11. India	
6. Korea	12. Indian	

page 85

Chapter 23

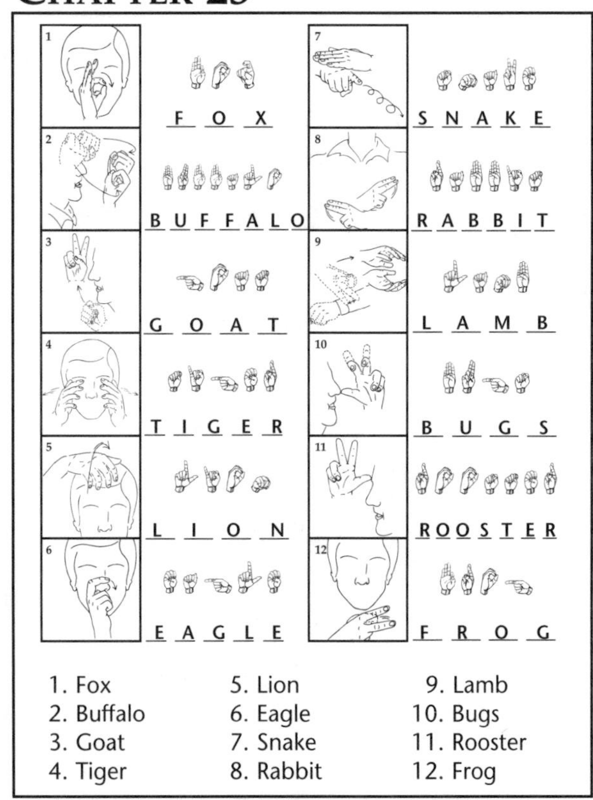

1. Fox	5. Lion	9. Lamb
2. Buffalo	6. Eagle	10. Bugs
3. Goat	7. Snake	11. Rooster
4. Tiger	8. Rabbit	12. Frog

page 86

A. **represents the worm crawling**
B. **shearing the sheep**
C. **representing the antlers**
D. **representing large ears**
E. **the large eyes of the owl**
F. **the bird's bill and wings**

7 sheep 4 B	8 bird 5 F	9 owl 1 E
10 mule 2 D	11 worm 3 A	12 moose 6 C

page 87

CHAPTER 24

1. A—Mission
2. A—Thee
3. C—Testament
4. B—Spirit
5. C—Sacrifice
6. A—Hallelujah
7. B—Passover
8. C—Commandments
9. A—Revival
10. B—Hanukkah
11. B—Gospel
12. C—Repent

page 88

13. C—Baptize
14. C—Minister
15. A—Soul
16. C—Christmas
17. B—Worship
18. C—Crucify
19. B—Resurrection
20. B—Grace
21. B—Vision
22. A—Verse
23. B—Bless
24. A—Holy

page 89

page 91

CHAPTER 25

1. C—12
2. C—Thousand
3. B—22
4. A—33
5. A—11
6. C—17
7. B—7th
8. A—1
9. A—7
10. A—28
11. C—20
12. B—$8.00

page 91

13. B—18
14. A—26
15. B—5 cents
16. B—14
17. A—34
18. C—25
19. C—21
20. A—100
21. A—4
22. C—10 cents
23. C—2/3
24. B—24

page 92

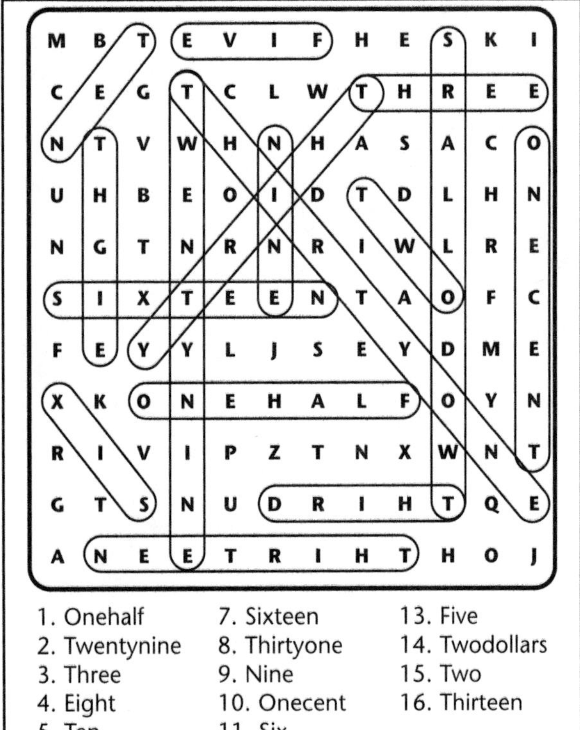

1. Onehalf
2. Twentynine
3. Three
4. Eight
5. Ten
6. Third
7. Sixteen
8. Thirtyone
9. Nine
10. Onecent
11. Six
12. Thirty
13. Five
14. Twodollars
15. Two
16. Thirteen

page 95